JOB INTERVIEWS

JOB INTERVIEWS

R.A. PADMANABHA RAO,
R. RAMESHCHANDRA

KALPAZ

Job Interviews

ISBN: 978-81-7835-884-0

Published in 2011 in India by
Kalpaz Publications
C-30, Satyawati Nagar,
Delhi-110052
E-mail: kalpaz@hotmail.com
Phone : 9212729499

Lasser Type Setting by: Rudra Computer Graphics, Delhi
Printed at : Chawla Offset Press, Delhi

This work is dedicated to R Sobha Devi

The unending Inspiration

Behind all our Success

On her 'Shashtpoorthi'

(61st bithday)

R.A. Padmanabha Rao

Ramesh Chandra Revuru

Contents

Foreword

Facing an interview

Having served in Government for over 4 decades, I feel that scouting new talent for a job is as challenging for the employer, as it is facing an interview for the candidate. Most of the aspiring candidates for Civil services dream of at least reaching the interview level. But at least 75% of the candidates who face the interview do not make it to the final selection list. This indicates the two different approaches to face an interview. While it may look seemingly easy for some, it poses challenges to the others.

An interview is a total test of ones personality. But first of all, you need to be called for an interview. That depends on how you fare in the written examinations.

R.A. Padmanabha Rao served All India Radio and Doordarsan for 3 decades and is a well known Telugu scholar. With his rich experience in Government and as an advisor to several institutions on the selection panels, he has dealt with the subject in a comprehensive manner.

The topics he has chosen and the way he has presented them will help candidates appearing for different interviews, to face the same with confidence leading to success. Similarly the 101 questions are exhaustive and interesting, though they mostly relate to soft ware sector.

I wish the publication all success.

Hyderabad
15th Jan 2011
Sankranti

K. PADMANABHAIAH, I.A.S
Former Home Secretary,
Govt. of India

1

Personality Development

"For starters, the odds against my 1930 birth taking place in the U.S.A. were at least 30 to 1. My being male nad white also removed huge obstacles that a majority of Americans then faced."

Warren Buffet

Birth is not our choice but a chance. One may born in a rich family another in a middle class and many in poor society. But by hard work one can build his future. If lady luck smiles he will be placed in a respected position.

Similarly career opportunities to an individual vary from person to person. Four brothers born to same parents may land up in different positions. Choosing a career and building a career are in the hands of an individual. Hard work and luck put together he can raise to highest position.

Mental and physical personality is God given, but one can improve it. Personality development can be attained through practice. Educational qualifications are important for career.

Acharyat padamadatte
Padam sishyaswamedhaya
Padam sadbramahachariblhayah
Padam kalakramenacha

Education is acquired in four stages – ¼ through teachers (Acharyas) – ¼ with his own brain – ¼ with co-students (Brahmachari) the rest over a period of time.

To enter into a profession one has to compete in examinations to get into personal interviews. If he is successful, he gets a job. This is like a snake and ladder game. One has to climb the ladder intelligently.

This book is divided into four major parts to suit the convenience of readers.

1. **Personality development.**
2. **Educational achievements.**
3. **Examinations for jobs.**
4. **Personal interview.**

This is PEEP into Job interviews. Let us make a move further.

PERSONALITY DEVELOPMENT

Personal charisma is what goes out and impresses others. Look at an industry leader like **Steve Jobs**. He is the CEO of Apple computers and has been voted by Fortune magazine as "CEO of the decade" When Steve Jobs returned to Apple in 1997 after a 12 year exile, the company was almost bankrupt. Thirteen Years later (2010), Apple has a market cap of 250 Billion USD. You could be lucky if you were a success with one industry but not four industries (Music - iTunes, Movies - Pixar, Computers – iPad & Telecom - iPhone) like with Steve Jobs. Between iPod (MP3 Player) announcement first and its official launch, Apple received 400 Million USD worth free publicity. That is what Steve is in a nut shell and Charisma is all about.

Mr. Nanthan Dorman mentions that "the Personality of the man is two – thirds and his intellect, his words are but one third. It is the real man, the personality of the man that runs throughout. The man who influences and casts his magic spell upon his fellow beings is a dynamo of power.

To have an overview of Personality Development a fivefold approach is needed.

1. *Social Development:* Show interest in other ideas. Display a positive attitude and know how to play up your positive side.
2. *Financial Development:* Try to improve your financial position. Financial discipline always will get respect in society.
3. *Mental Development:* Well informed and intellectuals are loved by society. Keep your eyes and ears open for increasing knowledge.

Read news papers, professional journals, fiction etc. Attend seminars, conferences and meetings. On an average one should read about 12 books in a year to improve your knowledge

4. *Physical Development:* Physical fitness, smartness and charming behavior always bring laurels. Outdoor recreation and exercise should become part of your daily schedule. Spare 30 minutes every day towards maintaining your physical fitness

5. *Spiritual Development:* Taking advantage of unfair methods is a bad habit. Self realization, meditation are important components.

Hence, personality traits in short are nothing but – individualism, sociability with strangers, ability to control strong emotion and impulse and personal achievement. Below is a beautiful letter written by US President Abraham Lincoln to his Son's teacher. Letter is all about personality development and personality development at a tender age.

Respected Teacher,

He will have to learn, I know, that all men are not just, all men are not true. But teach him also that for every scoundrel there is a hero; that for every selfish Politician, there is a dedicated leader...

Teach him for every enemy there is a friend, Steer him away from envy, if you can, teach him the secret of quiet laughter. Let him learn early that the bullies are the easiest to lick...

Teach him, if you can, the wonder of books...But also give him quiet time to ponder the eternal mystery of birds in the sky, bees in the sun, and the flowers on a green hillside. .

In the school teach him it is far honorable to fail than to cheat...Teach him to have faith in his own ideas, even if everyone tells him they are wrong...

Teach him to be gentle with gentle people, and tough with the tough.

Try to give my son the strength not to follow the crowd when everyone is getting on the band wagon...Teach him to listen to all men...but teach him also to filter all he hears on a screen of truth, and take only the good that comes through.

Teach him if you can how to laugh when he is sad...Teach him there is no shame in tears, Teach him to scoff at cynics and to beware of too much sweetness...Teach him to sell his brawn and brain to the highest bidders but never to put a price-tag on his heart and soul.

> Teach him to close his ears to a howling mob and to stand and fight if he thinks he's right. Treat him gently, but do not cuddle him, because only the test of fire makes fine steel.
>
> Let him have the courage to be impatient...let him have the patience to be brave. Teach him always to have sublime faith in himself, because then he will have sublime faith in mankind.
>
> *This is a big order, but see what you can do...He is such a fine little fellow, my son*!
>
> **Abraham Lincoln**

UNSELFISHNESS

Integrity and sincerity is the key to success. Every successful person has these two basic characters in life. Unselfishness is the driving force behind these qualities. Buddha and Jesus Christ preached these and followed in life. You may follow any faith. Every faith tells to be away from selfishness. It is easy to preach but difficult to practice. Islam leads the way in this regard. **Quran** (Holy script of Islam) presents the concept of **Zakat** (Alms giving). Zakat is one of the five pillars of Islam. It is giving of a portion of one's possesions to the needy in the form of charity.

Love, sincerity and patience are difficult to practice. But if we achieve them we are the happiest in the world. For Example in Hindu Mythology, **Lord Sri Rama** is epitome of success. His respect towards his parents is unparallel. His affection towards his younger brothers Laxman and Bharat is exemplary. We might argue that these are fictional and mythology. Let us take another real life example: **Mahatma Gandhi**. His love for his countrymen, patience in giving our country independence and sincerity towards the principles he believed are unquestionable. Hence, he became "Father" of our nation. One might again argue that both the examples are illogical as one relates to mythology and the other to public life. Let us now take a more recent and relevant example: **Narayana Murthy**, Chairman and Mentor of Infosys. Narayana Murthy's sincerity in business dealings, his love for IT industry and our country and patience are unfathomable.

Let us take a look at the 3 important lessons Narayana Murthy learnt in his life and career.

> ***NR Narayana Murthy (NRN) – Mentor, Infosys***
> ***3 Lessons learnt from his life and career***
>
> (1) He was a graduate student at IIT, Kanpur, in India when he learnt his first lesson of life. In 1968, he met with a computer

scientist who was on a sabbatical. NRN listened to the scientist addressing a large group of his students. Scientist in his lecture talked about the advancements in the field of computer science and how computers would change our future. That made NRN interested in computer sciences. (2) NRN was coming back to Mysore from a small town between former Yugoslavia and Bulgaria. He took a train from this town. In his coach there was a girl and a boy. Since NRN is fluent in French he quickly struck a conversation with the girl. They both talked how rigid the rule of the land was. Thinking NRN is criticizing communist Bulgaria government; Policemen came and take away NRN. NRN was then put in a jail.NRN was without food or water for more than 3 days. When NRN had almost lost hope on life, the jail doors open and he is escorted away in a freight train. While releasing him one of the guards tells him that he is lucky to come from a friendly country called India. Those events made NRN rethink about communism and capitalism. (3) The last event happened in 1990. After running the company (Infosys) for close to 10 years all the founders meet to discuss selling off the company for a sum of 1 Million dollars. Everyone of the seven founders (except NRN) present their point on why the company should be sold. NNR after listening to his colleagues said that if they were all decided on selling the company, he would buy the company and run it. The rest as they say is history. Infosys today is more than 4 Billion dollar company with 120,000 employees and is the 2nd largest IT company in India. Infosys has grown multi-fold to set an example for a lot of other countries

Concentration

Animals can be trained to act in a particular way. But most of them don't have memory and cannot remember. Human beings have the power of memory and concentration. India is known for ancient Rishis and Yogis who developed concentration techniques. It differs from one person to another. Art of **Sahasra Avadhana** in Telugu (Indian) language is based on concentration. The unique art is practiced in Telugu literature "only". Concentrating on 1000 poetical items at a time and being able to recite them back in the same order is the speciality of this art form. It is indeed a very rare feat to watch on stage. It can be cultivated and practiced. It is like developing compartments in the brain to remember. Another example is **Shankuntala Devi**, more popular as the mathematical wizard. She can answer 13 digit by 13 digit multiplication picked randomly in few seconds. We might wonder how that is possible. They are all contemporaries. They are also born like anyone else in ordinary families. The skill is developed by practice. Concentrating one item at a time is important. Concentration of the powers of the mind is important. It is difficult but not impossible in life. Nothing is impossible in life. This may appear like a sermon. But practice it. You will succeed. With the ever changing world one gets confused to remember things. Computers have eased our life style and made humans into their slaves. Almost everyone started heavily depend upon them. It is not that someone is against scientific developments and achievements but mental efficiency also is to be developed. A computer not matter how efficient can never parallel a human brain. Hence, use it and sharpen your brain. Improve your efficiency at work place. Be a Master and not a slave.

Key to success: Feltham, the great sociologist says "The greatest results in life are usually attained by simple means and exercise of ordinary qualities. These may for the most part be summed up in two: common sense and perseverance".

- Am I thinking enough?
- Am I satisfied with the quality of work?
- Am I working smart or hard?
- Have I ill-treated my neighbors or co-workers?
- Is my work praise worth?
- Have I achieved my goal?

Repeat these questions and answer them honestly and find out whether you are successful or not.

COMPASSION

If we are pure the world will be pure. The world changes with you. The person who has control over oneself cannot be overcome by anyone. Vicious thoughts generate hatred. You have to control such thoughts. Do not hate but spread the message of love. This will be your success in life. Grow in love and virtue. Outside world also will love you.

A teacher one day was talking to her students about compassion and caring for others. Teacher found one of her "**STAR**" student to be completely disinterested in her lecture.

Teacher stopped by and enquired why the student was lacking interest. To her surprise, student said that he strongly believed there is no scope for compassion in this cut throat competition. The world is relative and everything is bound to be compared. Comparison with the best and only losers talk about caring and compassion for others. Both agree to disagree and move forward.

Student then goes on to Join Microsoft after his graduation and does exceptionally well. He proves to the world that he is the best and Microsoft in retrospect rewards him by paying him the best compensation and promoting him. The STAR then goes on to star his own software company and does very well.

A few years pass by and one fine day the teacher has a visitor at her house. She cannot recognize the gentlemen at the door and requests the person to introduce himself. Visitor at her door is none other than her STAR student. He asks the teacher if she still remembers the conversation they both had few years back on compassion. Teacher nods her head and asks him what he has learnt in his life. Student then starts weeping in front of the teacher and asks her to pardon him. STAR then explains that in his madness for success he started treating everything as business including his family life. He started calculating the benefit to him from everything. Now his kid (10 year old) also started responding in the same fashion. It was then the realization bestowed on the importance of compassion in life

The teacher is none other than **Sudha Murthy**.

CHARACTER

According to religious faith, **Islam** is built on knowledge (Ilm) and Character (Akhlaq).

It is noted that one without knowledge and character is like an orphan who has lost both his parents.

Character building is Nation building. Sum total of all the impressions of your past life is the basis for character. Character is established by reacting to difficult situations. Habit is the second nature as well as the first nature. Why your friend is called a bad character? Why your parents advise you to avoid him? He has negative outlook and habits. Cultivating friendship with him may lead to troubles. A friend in need is a friend in deed. Repeated habits are character. You can reform the character through repeated habits. Build your character.

Depending on the character individuals are grouped into categories; The boss, The leader, The naturalist, The perfectionist, The Achiever, The Observer; The enthusiast; and The helper

ATTITUDE

- Your **attitude** not **aptitude** defines your **altitude** -Anonymous

Your attitude towards others is most important. If you have control over yourself anything outside cannot influence you. If we change the world will change. Be friendly to all. Show mercy to other in need. If people are happy we are also happy. Listen to the opinion of others. This attitudinal change is to be developed to be successful in life.

Think Yourself

There is an (in) famous story about thinking and thinking better than your opponent. According to this popular version, **NASA/USA** spent few million dollars inventing a pen that can write in space. Whereas, erstwhile **U.S.S.R** sent their astronauts to space with pencils and saved all the money.

You have enormous power to think. Your brain is well trained to give independent ideas. Sheepish mentality is developed in democracy. Leaders instigate people and they follow innocently. Act bravely and think properly. Great ancient thinkers and saints always believed in their power to think. Thought process is unending. Pure thoughts keep you healthy while impure thoughts make you feel bad. Mind is a devil's workshop. It depends upon how we engage it. Unemployed youth commit suicide for the simple reason that they are not successful in life. Watch the world around us. Take the example of a spider. It moves in the web which it has created. If the web is disturbed or spoiled it creates another. Alexander the great warrior took example from it. Never give up in life. Your parents, relatives and friends are the guiding force. Sometimes they may disappoint you or discourage you, but think yourself and act yourself. Believe in destiny. Hindu's holy book Bhagawat Geeta has lot of motivational quotes like "Karmanyevadhikarsthu maphaleshu kadachana" (Do your duty and be detached from the outcome).

LAUGH TOGETHER

> There is a famous joke about **Japanese** and **American** style of working. Not long ago, an American enterprise placed an order with a Japanese vendor for some electronic components. As part of the contract, American company told the Japanese vendor that they would not accept more than 1 defective piece for every 1000 pieces shipped. Order was placed for 50,000 pieces to be shipped within 4 months.
>
> In less than 4 months, American company received shipment from the Japanese vendor and it carried the below note"
>
> We fail to appreciate American practices but abiding by the contract we are shipping 50,000 '*quality certified*' pieces and a separate pack of 50 defective pieces"
>
> On a serious note, the story suggests the seriousness with which Japanese deal with their customers.

Laughing is unique for human beings. To laugh is good. To get others laugh is great. Unable to laugh is a disease. Human beings alone can laugh. Animals cannot laugh. Laugh and the world laughs with you. Laugh at yourself. Nature is kind to you. It has given you everything.

Humor should be a part of our life. Think of a speech you heard recently. If it is punched with humor you will never forget. Cultivate such ideas in you, while talking with friends.

Smile at others. You can do wonders with smiles. Mother Teresa approached the patients with smile and was able to do wonders. She is a living legend of our times. Caste, creed, religion are overcome by smile. She won over the hearts of millions of suffering people.

BE CONFIDENT

> Many hundreds of years ago in a small Indian town, a merchant had the misfortune of owing a large sum of money to the moneylender. The moneylender, who was old and ugly, fancied the merchant's beautiful daughter so he proposed a bargain. He said he would forgo the merchant's debt if he could marry the daughter. Both the merchant and his daughter were horrified by the proposal.
>
> The moneylender told them that he would put a black pebble and a white pebble into an empty bag. The girl would then have

to pick one pebble from the bag. If she picked the black pebble, she would become the moneylender's wife and her father's debt would be forgiven. If she picked the white pebble, she need not marry him and her father's debt would still be forgiven. But if she refused to pick a pebble, her father would be thrown into jail.

They were standing on a pebble-strewn path in the merchant's garden. As they talked, the moneylender bent over to pick up two pebbles. As he picked them up, the sharp-eyed girl noticed that he had picked up two black pebbles and put them into the bag. He then asked the girl to pick her pebble from the bag.

What would you have done if you were the girl? If you had to advise her, what would you have told her? Careful analysis would produce three possibilities:

(1) The girl should refuse to take a pebble.
(2) The girl should show that there were two black pebbles in the bag and expose the moneylender as a cheat.
(3) The girl should pick a black pebble and sacrifice herself in order to save her father from his debt and imprisonment.

The girl put her hand into the moneybag and drew out a pebble. Without looking at it, she fumbled and let it fall onto the pebble-strewn path where it immediately became lost among all the other pebbles.

"Oh, how clumsy of me," she said. "But never mind, if you look into the bag for the one that is left, you will be able to tell which pebble I picked."

Since the remaining pebble is black, it must be assumed that she had picked the white one. And since the moneylender dared not admit his dishonesty, the girl changed what seemed an impossible situation into an advantageous one.

The above story suggests that if you are confident you can win over difficult situations as well.

Young people with qualification and at an early age shy away from competitive exams (Civil Services, IIT & IIM or anything prestigious in their field of interest). An advice at this stage is necessary from friends, relatives and parents. They lack confidence. Confidence building exercise is most important. It can be done through counseling. Constant counseling from school level is important but found missing in our society today.

Most of the degrees acquired by students today are academic and don't develop their inherent talent. For few decades now, students enter engineering college because their parents want them to become Engineers OR pick a stream because their friends have opted. Selection of a stream at degreé Level is decided by the rank obtained at Intermediate level and the cutoff marks. Engineering course curriculum has been designed correctly but there is problem in implementation. Engineering courses in India introduces all streams (Civil, Computers, Mechanical, and Electronics) in the first year with an intention of providing an opportunity for the student to pick the specialization based on his/her interest. Is that the case today? The answer is NO. Engineering stream is decided in the first year itself at the time of admission.

Learning from books is important but understanding why, what and how gives abundant strengths. Self confidence is built through this inner learning. The abilities are like perennial water underground. They are to be tapped well.

LEARN FROM OTHERS

Vivek Pradhan was not a happy man. He was **Project Manager** in a **Software company** and still not entitled to air travel. It was not the prestige he sought; he had tried to reason with the admin person, it was the savings in time.

He opened his case and took out the laptop, determined to put the time to some good use.'

Are you from the software industry sir, 'the man beside him was staring appreciatively at the laptop. Vivek glanced briefly and mumbled in affirmation, handling the laptop now with exaggerated care and importance as if it were an expensive car.'

You people have brought so much advancement to the country, Sir. Today everything is getting computerized.

Thanks, 'smiled Vivek, turning around to give the man a look. He always found it difficult to resist appreciation.'

You people always amaze me, the man continued, 'You sit in an office and write something on a computer and it does so many big things outside.'

Vivek smiled deprecatingly. Innocence demanded reasoning not anger. "It is not as simple as that my friend. It is not just a question of writing a few lines. There is a lot of process that goes behind it."

It is complex, very complex.

It has to be. No wonder you people are so highly paid, came the reply.

This was not turning out as Vivek had thought. A hint of belligerence crept into his so far affable, persuasive tone. 'Everyone just sees the money. No one sees the amount of hard work we have to put in.'

'Let me give you an example. Take this train. The entire railway reservation system is computerized. You can book a **train ticket** between any two stations from any of the hundreds of computerized booking centres across the country. Thousands of transactions accessing a single database, at a time concurrently;

data integrity, locking, data security. Do you understand the complexity in designing and coding such a system?'

The man was awe struck; quite like a child at a planetarium. 'You design and code such things."

I used to, 'Vivek paused for effect, 'but now I am the Project Manager."

Oh!' sighed the man, as if the storm had passed over, 'so your life is easy now.'

This was like the last straw for Vivek. He retorted, 'Oh come on, does life ever get easy as you go up the ladder. Responsibility only brings more work. Design and coding! That is the easier part. Now I do not do it, but I am responsible for it and believe me, that is far more stressful. My job is to get the work done in time and with the highest quality. To tell you about the pressures, there is the customer at one end, always changing his requirements, the user at the other, wanting something else, and your boss, always expecting you to have finished it yesterday."

My friend,' he concluded triumphantly, 'you don't know what it is to be in the **Line of Fire**'.

The man sat back in his chair, his eyes closed as if in realisation. When he spoke after sometime, it was with a calm certainty that surprised Vivek.'

I know sir,....... I know what it is to be in the Line of Fire....... 'He was staring blankly, as if no passenger, no train existed, just a vast expanse of time.'

There were 30 of us when we were ordered to capture Point 4875 in the cover of the night. The enemy was firing from the top. There was no knowing where the next bullet was going to come from and for whom. In the morning when we finally hoisted the tricolour at the top only 4 of us were alive.'

'You are a...?'

'I am Subedar Sushant from 13 J&K Rifles on duty at Peak 4875 in Kargil. They tell me I have completed my term and can opt for a soft assignment. But, tell me sir, can one give up duty just because it makes life easier.On the dawn of that capture, one of my colleagues lay injured in the snow, open to enemy fire while we were hiding behind a bunker. It was my job to go and fetch that soldier to safety. But my Captain sahib refused me permission and went ahead himself. He said that the first pledge he had taken as a Gentleman Cadet was to put the safety and welfare of the nation foremost, followed by the safety and welfare of the men he commanded... ....his own personal safety came last, always and every time.."

He was killed as he shielded and brought that injured soldier into the bunker. Every morning thereafter, as we stood guard, I could see him taking all those bullets, which were actually meant for me.

I know sir....I know, what it is to be in the Line of Fire.'

Vivek looked at him in disbelief not sure of how to respond. Abruptly, he switched off the laptop. It seemed trivial, even insulting to edit a Word document in the presence of a man for whom valour and duty was a daily part of life; valour and sense of duty which he had so far attributed only to epical heroes. The train slowed down as it pulled into the station, and Subedar Sushant picked up his bags to alight.'

It was nice meeting you sir.'

Vivek fumbled with the handshake.

This hand... had climbed mountains, pressed the trigger, and hoisted the tricolour. Suddenly, as if by impulse, he stood up at attention and his right hand went up in an impromptu salute.

It was the least he felt he could do for the country.

PS: The Capt referred to here is Capt **Vikram Batra**, PVC **(Posthumous)**

> Live humbly, there are great people around us, let us learn from others!

We come across thousands of people in our life. Each one is different from others. Each one (painter, doctor, lawyer and so on) has excelled in life in one way or the other. Years of practice combined with detailed study and training made them great. Few may be born genius, child prodigies. But majority of them have achieved that status by sheer hard work. That could be you. Work on your strengths and weaknesses. Hard work and determination will help you achieve the greats achieved by others.

Own your mistake. That is the first principle to be followed. "Pramadho Dheemata mapi" (great people also are bound to do mistakes). Readily agree your mistake and own the mistake. It shows your humbleness. Apologize if mistake is done. Do not feel that it will reduce your reputation. It will create friendly atmosphere and people respect such people. If an error is on our part we should readily own it. Then only we will be successful in life.

> **Did you know?**
> **Jawaharlal Nehru** was interviewed on 22nd May 1964 on who his successor would be. Nehru's reply "*My life is not going to end so soon*". Jawaharlal Nehru died 5 days later on 27th May 1964 leaving the country grappling for a successor.

Negative Criticism

People are in the habit of criticizing others. They criticize the system, the administrative setup and the things around. They constantly search faults in others. It slowly becomes a habit in life and part of their nature. Positive outlook is always healthy. See good in every aspect of life. God has created the world in such a way that it lives in harmony and peace.

We have friends around us who criticize their teacher, friends, relatives, and neighbours. Always they find fault with them. We should avoid such negative thinking to succeed in life. Instead, we should think and aim to be the best. We loose noting by praise. Whereas the other person is so pleased and will be able to cooperate with us. Rarely do we come across someone who doesn't get pleased with praise. Be generous in praise which will fetch results. As they say, praise in public and reprimand in private. A Child who gets a pat from the elders does a good job when compared to continuous scolding.

> It is the success story of Ms. Malathi who was affected with polio at a tender age of 18 months. She lost sensation in her hands and legs. She spent more than 15 years in hospitals with Doctors, Operations and Physiotherapy. She was operated upon for 27 years. She did not lead a happy life like all other children during her childhood. She was admitted into the college. Her classroom is in first floor. She was inspired by her father to forget about the past and to invite future with full determination. He advised her to be unique in life and not to lead the life of common person. She took it as a challenge. The principal of the college acceded to her request to change the classroom to ground floor to suit her. She succeeded in life and participated in the games competition held for physically handicapped. She won Gold medals at National level games held once in two years. She competed and won medals at international games.
>
> Under the sports quota she got appointment as clerk in Syndicate Bank. She moves in a wheel chair with her face full of smile. It gives a positive message to all. Several such success stories can be narrated. Positive attitude is the only 'Mantra' for success.

Discipline

Doing ordinary things extraordinarily through proper actions is nothing but discipline. Discipline has so many advantages. Without discipline you cannot experience serenity. Achievement comes from disciplined action. Select a small project than a big one to strengthen your will power. Bad suggestions have a banal influence. Counter them. You have to master the art of dealing with time wasters.

"I have very little time already. Where is the time for worries?"- replied Sir Winston Churchill, Prime Minister of England when he was questioned by a Journalist about his worries during World War-II. We must keep our mind busy on constructive ideas. Life exists today. Yesterday is already gone. Tomorrow never comes.

"What is past is past, and that which is to come is not certain. Therefore man should do that which pertains to the present" said a Sanskrit poet. All realities are hidden in our present day, as yesterday is gone and tomorrow is only a dream.

2

Educational Pursuits : Learning for Earning

"Its recession when your neighbour loses his job; its depression when you lose yours."

- Harry Truman, 33rd US President

Graduation

You are expecting the results of your graduate degree in few months. This is the best time to plan for a career. You are at the threshold of entering the vast empire of career building. Unless you plan it properly you may be struck up at the bottom. New life starts with career. **Family life, social life, cultural life and the actual life starts with career.** Status of an individual depends on his career building. Respect he receives from the society is related to the profession and status he enjoys. Pure luck and astrology does not help. It gives a fillip. Students of Final year Degree has to concentrate more on exams as well as future plans for job hunt. The grade he acquires in the final exams is the criteria for selection. Total score shall be degree with I-class (60% marks on aggregate). That does not mean a candidate with 50% or less shall loose hopes on his future.

The lady luck waiting at the doorstep knocks the door. One should recognize her arrival and open the perfect door at an opportune time.

One should decide whether he shall opt for higher studies or a hunt for Job. It can be pursued simultaneously. He may think of pursuing higher studies abroad. Clear perception is needed. The dilemma at the initial stages shall be over come by firm determination. Three options are available. If economic status allows him to pursue higher studies abroad and he has availed the opportunities available and has competed in the relevant entrance tests, he can plan for it. It requires hard study and a thorough knowledge about higher education facilities available in different countries. He should get the counseling and approach proper persons. He shall select a better course for higher studies.

Career in Media

The media scene has changed in the past two decades with new policy of globalization. The present scenario is nearly 80000 News papers and periodicals, around 250 Radio stations (AIR) 400 radio Transmitters, 500 TV channels, 300 Private FM Radio stations, and community Radio stations are available. The print media in terms of readership covers almost the whole country. The viewership and reach of the channels is enormous. The all-round growth of media is strong. The entire humanity is in communication mode.

New communication systems are user friendly. It requires huge human resources. It includes men for management, content creation. production, presentation and distribution. The number of news channels has increased. It requires intelligent, well informed trained professionals. Further persons well equipped in Journalism, animation, printing, net work engineering, creative artists, writers and media managers are required.

There is a tremendous potential for jobs as well as self employment. More than specific academic degrees, personal qualities are required from the Prospective candidates. The requirements are hard working, self confidence, and well versed professionalism with excellent communication skills. Irrespective of their grades/ marks in degree courses, the professionals shall have to project themselves for actual working on the desk and at field work. It needs thorough knowledge of current events.

Mr. CK. Sardana, faculty member at Makhanlal Chaturvedi national university of Journalism and communication, Bhopal in an article in Employment news (dated 22-28 may 2010) mentions as below:

"They (the new entrants) must be able to think clearly, write clearly for print / electronic/ internet/ web media with an eye on the readers, viewers and users' requirements and their level of understanding. Their written 'copy' should mean value addition to its target audience".

Path to success

Media requires professionally competent and result oriented persons. The educational institutions training the students across the country play an important role. All of them come under the overall umbrella of media. Several universities are importing courses in Journalism, Radio and T.V. Makhanlal Chaturvedi national university of journalism and communication, Bhopal is prominent. The courses include advertising, public relations mass communications, computer science and applications.

Print Media

In print media several opportunities are available. Mainly – reporting, editing and management cadres. Management includes marketing, advertising, HR, Accounts and Circulation. The different positions in reporting wing are – Reporter/Senior Reporter/Chief Reporter/ Principal correspondent / Bureau chief etc. They are field based. Salary varies from management to management and experience of the person.

Editing wing carries posts like – Sub-Editor, Chief Sub-Editor, Deputy News Editor, News Editor, Editorial Advisor, Editor, Editor-in-Chief etc. With District editions coming up in regional language papers District in-charge position is created. The designations change from management to management (news paper/ periodical).

Management career includes advertising manager, Circulation manager, and Chief Manager etc.

Electronic Media

Radio and Doordarsan were prominent in Electronic media till 90's. With the advent of Private TV channels and web, internet and new media the scenario has completely changed. The positions in Electronic media are –

Technical / Production

Producer, Cameraman, Sound recordist, Broadcast/ video engineer, video recordist, video editor, makeup man, animator, floor manager, lighting director, technical director etc.

Creative Department

Script writer, visualizer, graphic designer, scenic designer, creative director etc.

News Media

Content monitor, content developer, content manager, web page developer, web page designer, web page manager etc.

Advertising Department

Account executive, client services executive, copy writer, visualizer, media planning executives, researchers, marketing managers, sales executives, event managers, graphic designers, creative director etc.

Public Relations :

Public relations is another field where large number of opportunities are available. A professional body, Public Relation society of India with 15 chapters all over the country with New Delhi as Head quarters is training different PR managers professionally. It conducts seminars, conferences, annual meetings to develop communication skills among PR professionals.

Corporate communications offer large career opportunities. It requires self confidence, hard work, foresight and far sight to shine as PR professionals. Besides Government Job opportunities, Public Sector and Private Sector provide several jobs in PR. They have varied designations - Information Asst., P.R.O., P.R. executive, corporate communication manager, General Manager (P.R), Executive Director – (corporate communications) etc.

The qualities required for effective communication in media are – Dedication, hard work, intelligence, resourcefulness, P.R. orientation and communication skills. On an average three lakh students come out of the universities with degrees in journalism and communications. The courses include video production, multi media, graphics, animation, entertainment communication, advertising, marketing, corporate communications, internet journalism, printing technology, environment communications and spiritual communication.

Indian institute of mass communication, New Delhi, Film & Television institute, Pune, Departments of Journalism of different universities, mass communication Departments of colleges teach Journalism. It has a mix of theory and practice. Training and internship are part of their studies. Attachment to daily news papers/weeklies/Radio & TV Channels is part of the course. Students prepare one documentation in Print / Video. Dissertation paper is compulsory on any given aspect.

Student with a degree has to decide himself the specific career for which he/she is suitable. He should have writing skills. The person must demonstrate his competence and usefulness in the organization. He should produce his published articles / Video productions to stand above all in the competition. It requires dedicated work from the day one he joins the course.

Career in Electronic Media

Electronic media is one of the fields that holds lot of promise in career planning. There is a boom in electronic media with many regional, national and international TV and Radio channels coming up. Presently we have 500 TV channels. Privatization of FM Radio by Information and Broadcasting Ministry has thrown open opportunities for youngsters.

Exciting Opportunities

Exciting opportunities are available in Electronic Media – Broadcasting production, animation, Video game design, digital and film editing etc. You can make your career creative and exciting. Video game design is one of the creative types in entertainment area. Jobs for these positions are competitive. One has to possess the basic degree to acquire the skills.

Specializations

Number of universities and other media institutions are offering degrees and diplomas in electronic media – camera, editing, anchoring, production and design etc. Knowledge about software programmes is necessary to enter the field. Degree in computer Graphics helps in getting a job like graphic designer, web designer and online marketing. Talent to develop CD Roms, Video games and website is necessary. Skills with soft ware programes as a digital artist will help to learn illustrations and graphic design techniques. Specialization in graphic and design skills keep him above the competitors.

In the film industry digital and editing opportunities are available. The film and television institute, Pune offers different courses in film and Television. Digital technology is used in Bollywood and Hollywood feature films. It requires film editing and digital technologies. Production and Editing opportunities are umpteen in television industry also. Editing is required in news broadcasts, TV sitcoms, and animated commercials or shows. Programmers at Film and Design schools have to cater to the needs of the youth. Hands on experience in design, editing and animation techniques are the need of the hour.

Electronic media is rewarding people with creative bent of mind and excellent communication skills. FM Radio has given several opportunities for Radio jockeying and production. Similarly TV Journalists, News analysts and TV artists are needed in the industry. They become popular artists.

Behind the scene Jobs

Equally interesting and lucrative Jobs are also available - such as handling cameras, sound recording, script writing, editing and production. There is a dearth of manpower. Dr. Pradeep Nair, a Research Scientist at Kidwai mass communication Research center MCRC of Jamiamilia Islamia, New Delhi mentions - **"That one needs to have apart from an innate aptitude for these jobs is sound knowledge and training."**

Universities and institutions offering these course are :

- Jamiamilia Islamia, New Delhi.
- Banglore University.
- Guru Jambheswar University, Hissar
- Devi Ahlya Bai University, Indore
- Makhanal Chaturvedi University of Journalism, Bhopal.
- Indian institute of Mass Communication, New Delhi.
- Symboisis Institute of Mass Communication, Pune.

They offer Degree and Diploma courses in Electronic media. They have their own syllabus.

Hotel Management

Chef is an expert in cooking. In ancient epics mention was made about Nala Chakravarthi & Bheemasena as experts in cooking. In modern era it is limited to some traditional families. Presently human resource development wing in Star hotels has increased. The main person in cooking is a Chef. With liberal economic policy in India the development in hotel industry has grown.

In hotel administration kitchen plays a pivotal role. The head of kitchen is Chef. Though Chef is part of Hotel management, in view of the modern needs it has become a specialized subject and a separate course for study. Culinary Arts as a food processing science came into existence. Important items in cooking, processing them, cooking and serving them to guests with care are a science called culinary arts. Quality in food items, preservation and distribution are the subjects taught in this course.

In America and Europe persons with these specializations have lot of demand and respect. Star hotels, Restaurants, Pubs and catering departments engage them and there is a good demand. During the recent years Chef Career in Naval ships has increased. Though culinary arts are part of hotel management there is variedness. House keeping, front office, food & beverages are part of hotel management course. In culinary arts all these subjects are part and parcel with more stress on kitchen. Here also the management principles, marketing, materials, French language, hotel law, human resource management, basic food hygiene, nutrition and food science and computer application are part of curriculum.

Besides the above, in culinary arts some more core items are studied. They study the food rules of FAO, international organization and HACCP. They study the following subjects at international standards – quality food making, serving them with dignity and Hospitality management. The course is structured to suit the needs of star hotels, international chain hotels, and their food requirements.

Those who have completed intermediate (+2) with 50% marks are eligible to do the course. Excluding the first year, the semester system is followed. One full semester is for internship in industry. In most of the cases the syllabus is oriented towards practicals for 70%. Important centers teaching culinary arts are:

1. Culinary Academy of India – Hyderabad.
2. College of Hospitality and Tourism – Guragon – Haryana
3. Amrapali Institute of Hotel Management, Haldwani (Nainital) UP.
4. International institute of culinary arts, New Delhi.
5. Mumbai College of Hotel Management and catering Technology – Mumbai.

In foreign countries –

- Lee cordon Blue Schools, North America.
- The art Institute system of schools.

In Countries like Australia, Argentina, France, Greece, Italy, Mexico, Philippines and Singapore the course is taught.

An exclusive website is available

www.chef2chef.net

Jobs in Tourism Sector

By the end of 2011 in Tourism and Hospitality sector alone an estimated of 18 to 24.8 million jobs will be available. World Tourism and Travel council Survey report mentions that 15000 trained persons are required immediately. 2700 Manager level posts will be Vacant. It is estimated that by 2020 Rs. 8.5 lack crore income generation from internal tourism sector will be raised.

Central and AP state Govt. has instituted in 2004 Dr. Y.S.R. National Institute of Tourism and Hotel Management to cater to the needs of trained personalat Hyderabad. The course curriculum is appreciated by International agencies.

NITHM Admission Schedule for 2011

Course	*Availability of Application*	*Exams*	*Joining Date*
B.B.A. (T.H)	April 2011	June 2011	1st July 2011
BHMCT	”	”	1st July 2011
M.B.A.	”	-	July
Certificate Course	”	-	July

www.nithm.ac.in

The institute is imparting Training in a better way. Many institutions like JNTU, Hyderabad; Osmania University, UNESCO, Indian Stastical Institute, Indian society for Training and Development etc. have entered into an MOU with this institute for training.

Courses offered :

(1) BBA Tourism and Hospitality through entrance test
Eligibility : Intermediate (+2)

(2) M.B.A. Tourism and Hospitality (2 years course)
Eligibility : Degree with 50 % marks
Admission through MAT, ICET, CAT score
Only 60 seats, course fees Rs. 1.25 laks.

(3) BHMBCT (Hotel Management and Catering Technology) 4 years course.
Eligibility : Intermediate (+2) Through Entrance Test
Course fees Rs 1,00,000/-

(4) Certificate courses of short duration are also available in Food production, House Keeping and Tour guiding.
Eligibility : 10th class.
Duration : 3 Months course.
Course fee RS. 5000.

(5) PG Diploma in Hospitality Education
Duration : 1 Year
Seats : 40

Assured Campus Placements

During NITHAM courses campus placements are done through interviews by different Organizations – Deloitte, APTDC, Infosys, Thomas cook, Singapore Air lines, GMR, Radisson, Indian School of Business, Malaysian Air lines & Internal Travel House.

In India alone 1.24 crores Jobs in Tourism sector are created. All over the world by 2014, Six Crore employment opportunities will be available as per the survey of World Tourism and travel council.

Job Guaranteed Professional Courses

Engineering, Medicine and Computer courses alone will not fetch jobs. Other courses also assure Job opportutinites Viz, CA, I.C.W.A., C.S., etc.

Commercial Companies need Chartered Accountants, Cost Accountants and Company Secretaries. Commerce Graduates with C.E.C Group in Intermediate (+2) can study these courses. Other students also can pursue.

Chartered Accountants

Certificate course in C.A. can be attempted with Intermediate. Institute of Chartered Accountants of India (I.C.I.A.) conducts exams in Three phases.

(1) Common proficiency test (CPT).
(2) Integrated professional competency course (IPCC)
(3) Assistantship (Final Course).

C.P.T.

Eligibility : Completion of second year Inter (+2) exams. They have to Register their names. The CPT exams are held in June and December. The exam is held in 4 subjects for 200 marks each.

IPCC

Candidates who have cleared CPT test are eligible to register. There are two parts – Group I and Group II. Candidate even with pass in one Group is eligible for Assistantship.

Assistantship

This is the final stage. Candidate has to register for 3 year article Assistantship with any CA. After completion of 2 ½ years Assistantship they can appear for the exams and get eligibility. After 6 months Assistantship he can join as Chartered Account in any company or can setup private practice.

Career Scope

Auditors, Tax consultants, Financial Consultants, Consultants in banking and Foreign Exchange markets. Branches of ICAI are functioning in all the states. Candidates can register with them. *www.icai.org*

ICWA

It is the best course for CEC candidates with Intermediate (+2). The Institute of Cost & Works Accountants of India (ICWA) train Cost and Management Accountants in the country in Three stages :

1. Foundation 2. Intermediate 3. Final.

Eligibility : Intermediate (+2) for foundation course - June / December.

The examination is in 4 papers

II Stage (Intermediate)

Eligibility: Degree or Pass in foundation course.

Exam in Two Parts - Group I and Group II

III Stage (Final) : Eligibility for Finals is Pass in Intermediate – stage exams.

8 papers + Essay in 500 words + 100 hours computer training and 15 days modular training. They have to complete Audit and Industrial Training for 6 Months.

Career Scope

Till the last decade, opportunities were limited to Mining, cement, jute production units etc. Now the scenario has completely changed. Jobs are offered in service sector, software industry, FMCG etc. There is lot of demand for eligible, trained and experienced Cost Accountants in the field. They can become Finance Directors, Financial controllers, Chief Accountant, Chief internal Auditor, Cost controller, Marketing Manager etc. They can run even private commercial units.

Tuition fees with study material: Rs. 7000/-

Oral Training fees with study material: Rs. 11,000/-

www.icwai.org

Company Secretary Course

To get appointment as Company Secretaries the completion of the course is a must. One can join the course after Inter (+2). After completion of foundation course, he can join in company secretary' Executive programme. Next is professional programme. Later pre-membership training is to be completed. Exams in June/December. Registration before 31st March or 30th September. Different branches are available in the country for registration.

www.icsi.edu.

SUCCESS STORY

Dr. K. Radha Krishnan

Another success story is of Dr. Radhakrishnan, Chairman ISRO, Bangalore. He won appreciation from none other than Dr. APJ Abdul Kalam, President of India for his active role in 'Chandrayan'. On the day of successful launch of Chandrayan he visited Guruvayoor, the famous temple in Kerala and performed Caranatic Music concert being a musician himself.

Dr. Radha Krishnan hails from a small village Iranjalakkuda near Trichur in Kerala. The village is in the national news recently for 100% computer knowledge persons in a village in India. His father Krishnamurthi Menon was Deputy Collector. Mother Ammini was District Educational Officer. Since both of them are will educated with modern ideology they encouraged young Radha Krishnan to pursue his studies according to his aptitude. He won several prizes during his school education.

His village is famous for Kathakali – a traditional dance format. He learnt Kathakali at a tender age of 7. Pursuing his studies he continued performing Kathakali on stage. His wish is to become a leading Kathakali Dancer. He could not continue performing Kathakali due to Rheumatic pains. Doctors advised him not to perform. He was consoled by his parents not to get disappointed. Then he opted for Carnatic music. He performed concerts on stage.

With regard to his studies, he had his primary education at his native place. He did his degree in Engineering from Kerala University. He got call letters from IBM and ISRO. His professor Dr. M.S.N. Potti advised him to opt for ISRO and blessed him that he will be a successful scientist. He had no second thought. His parents did not object to it. He entered ISRO as Avionics Engineer in 1971. He was relieved of rheumatic pains subsequently and doctors allowed him to perform Kath kali. So he continued Kathakali as well as Carnatic Music.

Turning point

ISRO is one of the leading institutions in India known for discipline and dedication. He never expected a Job in ISRO. He worked hard to be elevated to the highest post of Chairman ISRO in 2009. ISRO decided to open remote sensing centers across the country for research in weather, agriculture and oceanography. He was in-charge of the wing as Project Director in 1987. Later he was looking after the budget and finances of ISRO till 1997. He was responsible for a budget of Rs.

4000 crores and he feels proud of it. When he was establishing remote sensing centre at Kharagpur, he got interest in studying at IIT. He did research on 'Satellites – control over earth" and was awarded Ph.D.

He was Director of Oceanography Science Centre in 2000. Tsunami disturbed the coastal areas in 2004 and the role played by this centre was historical. It is renamed as Tsunami warning centre. He continued as its Director up to 2005. He was elevated as Vice-Chairman of Unesco committee to do research on oceans. Later he became Director of Remote Sensing Agency.

In 2007 he was elevated as Director VSSC at Trivandrum. Chandrayan is one of the proud and prestigious projects of India. When the project is being launched he was consulted by ISRO. His team prepared an instrument to test the surface on moon; which was part of moon craft rocket. The efforts made by him in "Chandrayan" made him Chairman, ISRO. The efforts for Chandrayan-II to be launched in 2013 will be a great wonder and the preparation is on the way under the dynamic leadership of Dr. Radhakrishnan. NASA and European Agency are coming forward to collaborate. An amount of Rs. 1300 crores is ear marked for the project. He feels it as his luck to serve in ISRO.

He is the first batch student of IIM, Bangalore in 1973. Among the seven Chairmen so for to ISRO, three are from Kerala Dr. Kasturi Rangan, Dr. Madhavan Nair and Dr. Radha Krishnan. Many youngsters from his village are inspired to join in Avionics Engineering. His wife is working with State Bank of Travancore. He is one of the rich personalities to be emulated by youngsters.

Law as a Career

Law graduates have different opportunities with economic liberalization in India. Law department is an important division in all companies. Top log global schools –

Cambridge University, Cambridge.
www.law.cam.ac.uk

Columbia University, New York
www.law.columbia.edu/

Harvard University – Massachusetts
www.law.harvard.edu

London School of Economics – London
www.lse.ac.uk/collections/law

New York University, New York
www.law.nyu.edu/

Oxford University, Oxford

www.law.ox.ac.uk

Peking University, Beijing

www.law.pku.edu.cn/llmp

Top Indian Law Schools

Nalsar University of Law, Hyderabad

www.nalsarlawuniv.ac.in

National Law Institute University, Bhopal

www.nllu.com

National Law University, Jodhpur

www.nlujodhpur.ac.in

NLSI University, Bangalore

www.nls.ac.in

NUJS – Kolkata

www.nujs.edu

Faculty of Law, Delhi University, Delhi

www.du.ac.in

ILS Law College, Pune

www.ils.law.edu

Indian Law Institute, Delhi

www.ilidelhi.org

Symbiosis Societies Law College, Pune

www.symlaw.ac.in

The Government Law College, Mumbai

www.gic.edu

Amity Law School, Delhi

www.amity.edu/als

Department of Legal Studies, Madras University, Chennai

www.unom.ac.in/legal.html

Dr. Ambedkar Law University, Chennai

www.tndlu.org

Faculty of Law Allahabad University, Allahabad

www.allduniv.ac.in

Demand for law graduates is increasing day by day. Here is a success story in law :

Success story of Justice S.H. Kapadia

He hails from a very very poor family. His parents could not feed the young children even with a single meal. They shared the meal with the children and there are days when the parents slept empty stomach after feeding the children. They conquered the hunger. He hails from a

Pharsi family near khetwadi – girgoan in Mumbai. He was born on 29th September 1947 (the year of Independence). His father was a clerk, who had two sons. The two sons while playing went up to Narayan Dhabholkar, where residential quarters of Bombay High Court are constructed. On their houses gold colour embossed name plates are attractive. When the boy saw them, his inner self told him that he should attain the post of High Court Judge. He told his younger brother that "one day I will also be a judge". The younger one did not take it seriously.

After few years the economic condition of the family improved. The boy completed the Degree and LLB. Due to family burden he stopped his studies. He joined as a clerk in GAGRET & Co. Later he moved as assistant to Mr. Feroz Damania, a leading lawyer. Feroz was like a God to labourers. He pleaded several cases for them and won. Family of the boy moved to Andheri in Mumbai. There the young boy – Kapadia fell in love with Shehanaz. It lead to their marriage.

Kapadia practiced at Bombay High Court from 1974. He was appointed as standing counsel for Income Tax Department and Municipal Corporation, Mumbai besides few more public sector undertakings. He studied Economics and commerce along with Law. His words with his younger brother came true in 1991. He was appointed as additional Judge for Bombay High court. He moved to the same High court Judges' Quarters. He was made regular Judge in the same High court in 1993. In 1999 he was appointed as a special Judge to investigate into Stock market scam. He submitted his report to Parliamentary committee and Reserve Bank of India.

He was elevated as Chief Justice of Uttara Khand High Courts on 5th August 2003. Within four months he became Judge of Supreme Court.

The memorable day in his life is on 10th May 2010 when he took our as Chief Justice of India. His wife and his two sons were happy to see him in that chair. He is Justice Sarosh Home Kapadia (Justice SH Kapadia).

His advice to youngsters is that young lawyers shall study Governments acts and think of changes in judiciary. Integrity and honesty are his real assets and he does not even own a car. Youngsters have to emulate him to come up in life.

Part - II

Research

Persons preferring to do research for the award of Ph.D. are very less in our country. The quality of research is not upto the mark. Many of the Researchers manipulate with the earlier dissertations. Dedication and devotion among researchers is decreasing day by day. Standard of research work compared to 2 to 3 decades back is less. In China the candidates completing Ph.D. every year is 50,000. In India it is only 8000. Out of 2.3 lakh engineers graduated in India in 2006, only 1000 did their research work for Ph.D.

In America and Britain top priority is given for research work. Industries and Universities exchange MOUs for research. It is the responsibility of the industry to provide technical support and funds for Research. Providing expertise and guidance is the responsibility of universities. That is why; foreign universities have reached highest levels in research when compared to India.

Competitive Spirit

With the arrival of foreign universities (at least 50 in number) the demand for quality teachers will grow. With the increase of engineering colleges in number and permission given to no. of institutions, the standards in education have come down. There is no check on better teaching and laboratory facilities. Though the student is spending lakhs of rupees on his education he is not getting better education due to lack of facilities. Corruption among these institutions is at the highest peak. In America the controlling agencies and supervisory bodies are more strict and they act with higher responsibility. They will not compromise with quality.

In India we have more than 490 Universities, (central, state universities and deemed universities, besides Institutions of National stature). There are 20,770 colleges affiliated to universities as on June 2009. Around 1.35 crore candidates graduate in a year. About 16,68,000 persons graduate in Engineering and Architecture. It is the question of quality and not quantity. Only 15 to 25% have employment skills. The research findings of NASSCOM and MCKINSY revealed the above facts.

Better Education at Your Door Step

Mr. Niyogi did his Electrical Engineering with 80% marks. Miss. Sunita did her MBA Finance with Distinction. But the opportunities for them to be absorbed in any job have not come. They tried for more than 18 months and did some of the software courses. This is the scenario with lakhs of youngsters in India. Middle class parents have sacrificed their salaries, comforts and entire life to provide their children with good education. They are worried at the situation of their children who are yet to settle in life. They even send their children to UK, USA and Australia for higher studies by spending lot of money as fees. The Govt. of India has introduced a bill - Foreign universities bill in parliament. It has shown a ray of hope among the students.

With the arrival of foreign universities in India, better education facilities will be available. It will increase the standard of education and employment opportunities. If it materializes the dreams of middle class parents will come true.

Quality in education

The education which we impart to our students in the educational institutions has no relevance to the development in different fields and commerce and trade. Syllabus of some of the courses is outdated. In American Universities the syllabus is revised with latest developments in the area. Specialized courses to suit the requirements of the industries are introduced every year. Internship is compulsory for every student. By the time he completes his course he will be a skilled person to suit the requirements of the industry. The same standards will be maintained if foreign universities enter into our educational system.

Let us go through an analysis of students going abroad for foreign education. It is only a sample survey for a year on an average (2009).

Country	*Country wide persons going abroad*	*Only from Andhra Pradesh*
U.S.A.	60,000	18,000
U.K.	20,000	5,000
Australia	20,000	5,000
Canada	8,000	1,000

The tuition fees charged at different universities for different courses per year in Rupees is as follows:

The analysis show how our students migrate to foreign land for higher studies with the fond hope of getting better education and job opportunities.

Country	*MBA*	*M.S*
USA	10 to 22 Lakhs	5 to 35 Lakhs
UK(One year course)	7 to 16 Lakhs	6.5 to 13 Lakhs
Australia	11 to 12.5 lakhs	8 to 16 lakhs
Canada	8 lakhs	8.5 to 9.5 lakhs

SUCCESS STORY

All branches of education are equal, not only engineering. A student of veterinary science got recognition in U.S.A. Mr. V.K. Sing completed his graduation in veterinary sciences at S.V. Veterinary College, Tirupati. He did his post graduation also at Tirupati. He got three gold medals in Degree besides one in PG and one for Ph.D. Every one discouraged him from joining post graduation since it may not fetch him good job. Govt. Jobs in Andhra Pradesh for an M.V.Sc., graduate are very less. Private practice of animal Husbandry Postgraduate is wasting time since our country is not well developed. Even if an animal is sick, Govt. Veterinary hospitals will cure them. V.K. has a research bent of mind. He has done research and his papers were published in International Science Magazines. Prof. Roman. R. Ganta from U.S.A. appreciated the unique research work done by V.K. and discussed with him about the opportunities available at the Kansas university and encouraged him to pursue further research studies. Fellowship was offered at Kansas University. With determination for Research, V.K. decided to go abroad. He went to U.S. in 2002. After completion of his research on ticks, one kind of bugs he got recognition. He is presently Director, central state research institute at OMHA city (U.S). His wife Dr. Sujata a Ph.D in agricultural sciences works for the same institute on a research project. V.K's father Sri. S. Munisundaram (Tirupati), an established Telugu writer in Andhra Pradesh is proud of his youngest son. The success story is an example for a student with higher goals. He has set an example by continuing his research and presently he is well placed.

When we sum up the above success story the following points emerge:

- *Determination of the candidate.*
- *Family support.*
- *Specialization in the field.*

- *Initial hick ups.*
- *Prospects in any system of medicine (Animal Husbandry)*
- *Luck combined with hard work.*

TIPS FOR TOFEL

To get admission into foreign university courses, TOFEL is important. America, Britain, Canada and other 130 countries are accepting TOFEL score. It is necessary to understand the system of TOFEL. The examination is mainly meant for those whose mother tongue is other than English. There are four sections in the examination.

1. Reading, 2. Writing, 3. Listening and 4. Speaking. If we increase our aptitude towards reading and listening the other two are easy.

Reading. Recorded lessons by English lecturers and Pod casts are to be listened carefully. It is better to go through the websites of different foreign universities. Listen to NDTV, BBC, CNN and other NEWS channels. Similarly lot of reading material is available in popular websites. Wikipidea.org is an important site. Chatting with friends of English speaking countries and discussions with them will help in learning English.

Writing. Behave like a journalist by yourself. Note down the speeches of different personalities and prepare the summary. Use vocabulary and flash cards. Behave like a contestant participating in a vocabulary quiz show. You tube is a best source – www.youtube.com/TOFEL TV. We get lot of tips and guidance from the candidates who appeared for TOFEL and English language instructors.

Writing is an art. Writing effectively and exactly is the main crux of the problem. For example read an article on the same subject, take listening material and then prepare a summary. Then explain the similarities and adversaries in the article. In that direction collect reading and listening material on the same subject. Practice to summarize it in one minute oral summary or outline. It shall be 150 to 225 words **www.tofelgoanywhere.org** provide tips watch, video clips and model questions. Download them and prepare effectively for the TOFEL.

Paraphrasing and summarizing texts are to be practiced. Use charts and outlines. Learn the techniques of quick reading. Practice on your computer the questions on reading. Techniques of listening are also important. After listening the entire text understand the main idea. Similarly major points and other points are to be grasped.

Listening. Speakers attitude is to observed and that is the practical understanding of listening. Why the speech ? With what authority the speaker is talking? The correlation between the ideology is to be understood. Then only we know the negative side and the essence of the speech.

Take a small article from Newspaper/ Magazine/ Text books/ Internet and read it loudly. Prepare two or three questions from the article. Try to get answers by talking to your speaking partner. Learn to talk in one minute about the entire subject. Tell your opinion on the subject. Discuss the problem and find a solution.

Pronunciation

The way of talking is another aspect. Observe the way of taking by Americans and British. Practice talking in slow motion. Observe the way how they pronounce the letters T, D, K, P. Understand the coordinated movement of lower lip and teeth. You may not be talking like a native even after good practice. But they understand when you talk.

JOB Opportunities in Economics

Economics is a social science. Production of goods, consumption, distribution into market and allied services come under Economics. Economics deals with Raw material, land, capital, technology and labour. Study of demand and supply, exchange rates, business trends, taxation, employment rates, costing are the subjects in Economics. The world economic scenario will be studied as an economist. Students of economics can enter the fields of Business and Education in Govt. and private sectors. The financial planning is necessary for any field. For Ex: Education, family, health, law, politics, religion social organizations, wars etc.

Career in Economics

There are better opportunities for students of Economics. For all developmental activities in Govt. finance is the main criteria. The political agenda of a country is dependent on financial aspects. Economists have teaching and research opportunities in India and abroad. Colleges, Universities, Management Institutes provide employment. Those who qualify in NET can join as lecturers in Colleges and Universities. National level organizations like Reserve Bank of India, National Council of Applied economic research (New Delhi), Institute of applied Manpower Research Analysis and Policy provide Employment Potential. World Bank, European Economic Commission contain specialists in Economics. Economists are consulted in providing financial help by World Bank to the backward countries.

Union Public Service Commission conducts every year examinations for Indian Economic Service (IES). Working in Reserve Bank of India is a great opportunity. Similarly Employment in all banks is open for graduates of Economics. Opportunities in industries and commerce are plenty.

Person with economics Masters Degree can join as Agricultural Scientist in Agricultural Research Organization. Opportunities in Business magazines, Journals, Business Journalism and Journalism are plenty across the country.

Electronic and print media need lot of economists. Graduates in Economics get jobs in Finance, Banking, Insurance, Stock Markets, Sales and Marketing. Specialization in economics can help to join in media. The educational facilities in economics are available in colleges and Universities. Besides regular course, correspondence courses are also available. M.Sc., (Economics) is awarded by Anna University, Birla Institute of Technology and Sciences and Chatrapati Sahuji Maharaj Universities. M.Phil and Ph.D. courses are offered as research work. Delhi school of Economics, Jawaharlal Nehru University (JNU), Banaras Hindu University offer courses in Economics at post graduate level besides M.Phil., and Ph.D. Gohkale Institute of Politics and Economics, Pune offer MM, M.Phil., Ph.D. Courses. Indiragandhi Institute of Development Research, Mumbai (IGIDR) offer 2 years M.Phil., and 4 year Ph.D. courses. B.Tech and M.Tech cources are also available in Economics.

Other Institutions

Anna university (Chennai), School of Economics (Chennai), Aligarh Muslim University (Aligarh), Andhra University (Waltair), Kolkata University, Delhi University, University of Hyderabad, Jadhawpur University, JNU Delhi, Lucknow University, Madras University, Madurai Kamaraj University, Mumbai University, Pune University, and the Indian statistical institute offer courses in Economics. Indian council of social sciences provides research facilities in economics. In economics there are 4 branches – Home Economics, Indian Economics, Industrial Economics, and International Business & Finance.

Business Economics

Post Graduates of Business Economics can do research in specialized fields like Marketing, Industries, Cost and prices, Macro economics and environment. 13 universities in India offer special courses in Economics. Master of Business Economics (M.A. Business Economics) degree is also awarded.

Development Economics

To solve problems in finance and to develop the country this Branch is introduced. Only 6 Universities in India offer this specialized course. Rural development is nation development. With this spirit Institutes of Rural development in different states have been started. Ministry of Rural development promoted National Institute for Rural development at Hyderabad (NIRD). Masters Degree in Rural Economics and Rural Development is introduced in 12 universities.

Econometrics

Mathematics and Economics combined together is Econometrics. Presently only 4 universities in India teach econometrics. Madras University, Pondicherry University, Rani Durgavati University, Sri Venkateswara University, Tirupati and Indian Statistical Institute offer this course. Number of opportunities are available for economists in teaching field as well as media.

Tips for success

Positive attitude: While attempting for a job do not be pessimistic. If you always think that you are unemployed your confidence will shake. Unemployment is a phase in your life and you shall be able to overcome that temporary phase. With positive attitude and thorough hard work one should attempt. Success reaches him.

Defeat and Fear: Fear is behind a defeat. Alexander did not loose hopes in conquering his enemies. Failure is a stepping stone for success. Confidence is more important in any walk of life. Efforts shall supplement confidence. If you start fearing you will be loosing the opportunities. In case you are deeply immersed in personal failures and attempt, definitely you will not succeed. Failure and success are not in our hands. Not getting call letter and failure in interview is part of the game. One who attempts without any fear is sure to succeed.

Don't be proud

In case you are in the midst of a problem and in need of a help don't feel shy to ask for help. Discuss the problem with them. In case you are indifferent the opinion about you may change. Such type of behaviour is needed to a certain extent but it shall not exceed limits. People around you in the society may be willing to help you in getting the job. Instead of proceeding with confidence request them for help. Identify the persons and make an earnest request for help.

New Skills

Acquisition of new skills will give you strength. People more intelligent and more qualified are competing with you. Do not forget the basic fact. It is not easy to overcome them unless you acquire new skills required for the job - technical or academic. Learning more about the job and its requirements is most important. With the invention of computer knowledge the entire world is in a web. Acquire more skills with ease. **Be a student for ever.** Acquisition of mere degrees from universities with high percentage of marks is not only the criteria, though it is essential. In a competitive world your basic knowledge + something more will help you.

Career Planning

What is career? Occupational psychologists describe it as a ladder of occupations showing upward mobility. After completion of education one joins an occupation initially and moves up further throughout his employment. It can be from one occupation to the other or in the same job. The process is known as CAREER.

Career planning is setting up an ideal and an appropriate career based on the course of studies. It shall commensurate with the basic aptitudes, personality traits, work style and work preferences. It is again based on acquired skills, self confidence, adjustment level and emotional intelligence levels etc.

Steps in career planning

(a) Gain better understanding of aptitudes, intrinsic interests, personality traits, self confidence, adjustment status and psychological hurdles affecting careers.
(b) Find out the career related aptitudes.
(c) Sort out matching fields of future studies.
(d) Discover occupations that match the course of studies and other competencies.
(e) Know the people working in such careers.
(f) Know relative circumstances and demands to execute it.
(g) Know the work preferences in such occupation.
(h) Know the personality traits facilitating such occupations.
(i) Know other competencies needed in the work environment.

(j) Visualize whether these adjustments will result in stress or satisfaction.

(k) In case of readjustment work out transferable skills.

(l) Know your emotional intelligence levels.

The next step is to analyze compiled information about occupational options. It includes working environment and conditions, training and other qualifications, advancement opportunities, employment trends, future job outlook, compensation and other incentives.

Decision making is another step. Taking the experience of a career counselor is important. Execute the career plan by undergoing the course of studies - taking effective steps. If any readjustment is warranted it is another step.

Significant factors which play prominent role in career planning and development are to be understood. Aptitudes are pointers for symptomatic performances. They determine the attainment levels as well as types of activities. Every occupation requires different levels of aptitudes.

Important aspects

- Competition with excellence and success.
- Unique achievement.
- Long term involvement.

Personality patterns will also decide the selection choice. Balanced personality will go a long way in deciding the career matching. Extrovert personalities are preferred for jobs involving people's interactions. Introverts are considered in fewer interactions with people. Neurotic patterns in general are suited where quick actions are needed. In case the personality traits do not match with the job, it may lead to problems in execution. This personality measurement is done through personality inventories and projective techniques.

Confidence Level

Lack of self confidence is the cause of failures. One may be successful in academic records but self confidence is more pivotal. The quality of mind or spirit will enable the person to face difficulties. It is the indicator of self confidence. Generally lack of competence, physical disabilities, inferiority complex and negative attitudes are responsible for low confidence. One has to overcome this weakness in building up self confidence.

Emotional intelligence :

Dr. S.S. Chadda, Career counselor, Chandigarh suggests the following:

(a) Self awareness
(b) Management of emotions
(c) Self motivation
(d) Recognizing other's emotions

Emotional intelligence (E.Q) is of paramount importance in giving better performances. Similarly the work preferences are associated with occupations. Young people suffer from psychological hurdles. Lack of knowledge of aptitudes and related fields of careers, lack of concentration, feelings of depression, lack of self confidence and motivation, uncontrolled temper, nervousness, sexual conflicts, inferiority complexes, fears and worries about financial support, parental indifference and lack of rapport with them are some of the problems. Such hurdles contribute negatively in educational success. Chance factors also contribute.

The best career plan may not meet its desired goals due to factors beyond our control – Natural calamities, dynamic technological advances etc. Such eventualities result in creation of new avenues and at the same time restrict expansion in existing career fields.

Mental and physical abilities, work preferences, personality make up, aptitudes, attitudes and emotional intelligences are important factors in career planning. Some occupations demand special types of physical abilities. For example, Military and Police departments require persons who can work for long rounds, active movement, physical fitness etc. So one must be aware of his own strengths and weakness in career planning. Instead of wasting one's time in gauging his physical fitness, at the initial stage itself, he can choose his field depending on his physical traits. Luck and hard work are two important factors.

Part – III

Bio Data :

The Bio data along with a covering letter is to be sent if there is no prescribed application format. Model Bio – Data Format:

1. Name in Full:
2. Address : Permanent.
   Temporary
   Phone No. with STD code: 0
   Mobile No.: 09
3. Date of birth & Age as on 1.1.2011 :
4. Sex : Male / Female
5. Married / Unmarried :
6. Languages : Spoken, Read, Writing
7. Educational Qualifications: 10 + 2 on wards

Degree	% of Marks	Year	University
BA/BSC/Bcom			
MA/MSC/Mcom			
Ph.D.			
P.G. Diplomas			

8. Awards, medals, Prizes
9. Research Projects / Papers published if any.
10. Previous Employment in chronological order indicating year

Designation	Office / Institute	from – to	pay

11. Responsibility in present job :
12. Hobbies :
13. Salary expected :
14. Two references :

No.	Name	Designation & Address	Phone
1.			
2.			

15. Your suitability for the job. [Separate note be enclosed]

Enclosures :

Place: Signature

Date :

Filling up Application Form :

Do's

- If application format is given, follow the instructions carefully.
- If it is to be filled in Black ink, fill it.
- If it is to be within the boxes do it accordingly.
- Get it typed if printed format in not available.
- Send original application form.
- Send latest /Colour passport size photograph.
- Fill up all the columns with Yes / No
- Check up after filling.
- Keep a copy of the filled in application.
- Sign the application.

Don'ts :

- Don't use your present office letter head.
- Don't mention names of high profile officers you know as references.
- If your close relatives are highly placed, don't try to impress upon the company.
- **Don't forget to put signature.**
- Bio data should not be lengthy.
- Enclosures not to exceed 5 to 6.
- Don't give wrong information.
- Don't leave the columns blank.

Real story

Mr. Shankar applied for U.P.S.C. post and has sent his application with out signature. Two days later he identified the mistake. He has not signed immediately after filling the application since the time was not auspicious (Rahu Kalam – Bad Time). In his hurry he has posted without signature and realised it later. He has sent in another application with the signature after the last date. Commission did not accept it.

Do's for UPSC Posts

A. Before submitting the filled in application form, ensure

- That you have correctly indicated the name and year of the examination for which you are applying.
- That you have filled all the relevant columns correctly.
- To change responses, if required, you have erased darkened circles completely.

- That you have pasted your photograph firmly at the space provided.
- That you have pasted firmly the CRF Stamp (if applicable) you should paste only one CRF stamp of requisite denomination and get it cancelled from the post office of purchase.
- That you have mentioned correctly the commission's notice No. and date as published in the employment news/Rozgar samachar.
- That you have signed the declaration and mentioned the date and place of mailing the form.
- That you are using the pre-addressed envelope supplied to mail the application form and acknowledgment card. No other documents or copies of certificates or self-addressed envelopes are required to be sent long with the application form.
- That you have read the relevant examination rules and instructions before filling up the form.
- That you have noted down separately and kept for record and future reference the eight digit form number printed under the bar-code and entered the same correctly in the acknowledgement card.
- Also do ensure that you dispatched the form sufficiently in advance to ensure that it reaches the commission office before the prescribed closing date.

Don'ts

- Do not use the photocopy of the application form.
- Do not make any stray marks on the form.
- Do not staple, pin, mutilate, scribble, tear, or wet the form.
- Do not send enclosures (like certificates, etc.) with your form Only acknowledgement card is necessary, if application is sent by post.

References :

In the application candidate has to mention two references. Think for a while before you fill the form.

The following references can be given:

- Senior officials in the State Govt./ Central Govt.
- Professors / Academicians of your University.
- Names of MLA/MP/ Minister of **your area to be avoided**
- Names of Cine Stars to be avoided.
- Names of close relatives, (highly placed) are to be avoided.
- Names of your previous employer can be given.

The recruiting agency will check up with the references which you have mentioned. The address and telephone numbers given are to be latest.

Mere mention of the name as reference does not help. The person under reference shall know about you. He shall be able to tell about your credentials. Do not take it light. It is a serious subject where the recruiting body wants to assess your candidature from the elders whom you have given as reference. Minimum of two names are necessary with full particulars.

If you are giving the reference of your previous boss where you worked, think for a while whether you have left the job with the consent of the organization.

If you do not have the full address, telephone number of the references mere mention of Dr. K.A. Bhat, Pandara Road, New Delhi will not help. Give full postal address, land line, mobile and e-mail Id.

3

Examinations in Search of Talent

"If we know what we know, we will be twice our size."
-HEWLETT PACKARD, CEO

To build up a career one has to undergo several tests in life. Most of the employers conduct written tests to screen thousands of applicants. One has to be on the look out and qualify himself in the written test. We are providing basic material for such examinations. Details can be searched on different websites.

Union Public Service Commission

Historical Background

Indianisation of the superior Civil Services became one of the major demands of the political movement compelling the British Indian Government to consider setting up of a Public Service Commission for recruitment to its services in the territory. The first public service commission was set up on October 1st, 1926. However, its limited advisory functions failed to satisfy the peoples aspirations and the continued stress on this aspect by the leaders of our freedom movement resulted in the setting up of the Federal Public Service Commission under the Government of India Act 1935. Under this Act, for the first time, provision was also made for the formation of Public Service Commissions at the provincial level.

The Constituent Assembly, after independence, saw the need for giving a secure and autonomous status to Public Service Commission both at Federal and Provincial levels for ensuring unbiased recruitment to Civil Services as also for protection of service interests. With the promulgation of the new Constitution for Independent India on 26th January, 1950, the Federal Public Service Commission was accorded a constitutional status as an autonomous entity and given the title –

Union Public Service Commission

Constitutional Provisions :

The Union Public Service Commission has been established under Article 315 of the Constitution of India. The Commission consists of a Chairman and ten Members.

Present Members as on Jan. 2011:

Chairman Prof. D.P. Agarwal

1. Prof. K. S. Chalam,
2. Smt. Shashi Uban Tripathi
3. Prof. Purushottam Agarwal
4. Dr. K.K. Paul
5. Lt. Gen (Rtd) Nirbhay Sharma
6. Shri I. M. G Khan
7. Shri Prashanta Kumar Mishra
8. Shri Vijay Singh
9. Smt. Rajni Razdan
10. ....vacant.

The terms and conditions of service of Chairman and Members of the Commission are governed by the Union Public Service Commission (Members) Regulations, 1969.

The Union Public Service Commission has been entrusted with the following duties and role under the Constitution:

1. Recruitment to services and posts under the Union through conduct of competitive examinations;
2. Recruitment to services and posts under the Central Government by Selection through Interviews;
3. Advising on the suitability of officers for appointment on promotion as well as transfer-on-deputation;
4. Advising the Government on all matters relating to methods of Recruitment to various services and posts;
5. Disciplinary cases relating to different civil services; and
6. Miscellaneous matters relating to grant of extra ordinary pensions, reimbursement of legal expenses etc.

The major role played by the Commission is to select persons to man the various Central Civil Services and Posts and the Services common to the Union and States (viz. All-India Services).

EXPENSES OF PUBLIC SERVICE COMMISSIONS

The expenses of the Union or a State Public Service Commission, including any salaries, allowances and pensions payable to or in respect of the members or staff of the Commission, shall be charged on the consolidated Fund of India or, as the case may be, the Consolidated Fund of the State.

RECRUITMENT TO VARIOUS SERVICES AND POSTS

Under Article 320 of the Constitution of India, the Commission are, inter-alia, required to be consulted on all matters relating to recruitment to civil services and posts.

RECRUITMENT is made by one of the following three methods.

1. Direct Recruitment;
2. Promotion; and
3. Transfer

DIRECT RECRUITMENT is conducted broadly under the following two methods:

1. Recruitment by competitive examination.
2. Recruitment by selection through interview.

RECRUITMENT BY COMPETITIVE EXAMINATION

Under the Constitution one of the functions of the Commission is to conduct examinations for appointment to Civil Services/ Posts of the Union. In addition, competitive examinations are also held by the Commission under arrangement with the Ministry of Defence for entry to certain Defence Services, through the National Defence Academy, Indian Military Academy, Naval Academy, Air Force Academy and the Officers Training Academy.

The Commission usually conducts over a dozen examinations every year on an all India basis. These include Examinations for recruitment to services/ posts in various fields, such as Civil services, Engineering, Medical and Forest Service, etc.

At present the Union Public Service Commission conduct their examinations at numerous venues spread over 42 regular centers throughout the country.

RECRUITMENT BY SELECTION

Recruitment by Selection is made by the following methods:

1. By Interview Only
2. By Recruitment Test Followed By Interview.

BY INTERVIEW ONLY

Where the number of applicants is very large, it is not practicable to call for Interview all the applicants who fulfill the minimum eligibility conditions prescribed. The Commission, therefore, shortlist the candidates to be called for the interview on the basis of certain pre-determined criteria related to the job. A large number of recruitment cases is handled by the Commission by the method (1) above.

BY WRITTEN TEST FOLLOWED BY INTERVIEW

In this category, there are two types of procedure followed:

(a) An objective-type written and/or practical test to test the skill of the candidates followed by Interview. The final selection being decided by interview, aided by the performance of the candidates in the written test and/or practical test.

(b) An objective-type written and/or practical test to screen candidates to be called for interview, the final selection being decided by interview only.

ALL INDIA SERVICES

The All India Services Act, 1951 and Rules and Regulations framed there under regulate the recruitment and conditions of service in respect of the All India Services viz. Indian Administrative Service, Indian Police Service and Indian Forest Service.

As far as direct recruitment to the Indian Administrative Service and Indian Police Service Examination are concerned, it is done through the Civil Services Examination and for the Indian Forest Service through the Indian Forest Service Examination held by the Commission.

The relevant Rules and Regulations provide that 33% of the vacancies in the IAS/IPS/IFS should be filled by promotion from amongst the officers of the State Service in consultation with Commission. The Selection Committee presided over by Chairman/ Member of the Commission consist of senior Government representative of the Central Government and the State.

MECHANISATION – PROJECT SAMPERA

The Commission have recently undertaken a project called "SAMPERA" (Screening and Mechanised Processing of Examination and Recruitment Applications). A simplified single sheet common application form for all the examinations has been devised which will be scanned by using OMR/ICR technology. The implementation of this project will mainly help in high speed scanning of data from forms eliminating manual entry. Other benefits will be accurate and faster generation of Admit Cards, Attendance lists with photo replica and signature facsimile of each candidate, and Error – free list of doubtful cases. The main aim of this project is to cope with the increasing volume of applications through innovations and mechanized handling so as to reduce the processing time and send communications faster to minimized errors. The cases of impersonation/malpractices will also be eliminated and wasteful expenditure will be reduced.

RECRUITMENT RULES

In accordance with the provisions contained in Article 320 of the constitution read with the provisions of Union public service commission (Exemption from Consultation) Regulations 1958, Recruitment, Rules of all Group "A" and Group "B" posts in various Ministers/Departments of Government of India are required to be framed in Consultation with the commission. Consultation with the commission is also necessary for framing/amending recruitment rules certain categories of posts under the employee's state insurance corporation, The Delhi Municipal Corporation, the New Delhi Municipal Council, Employees provident fund organization etc. under the relevant Acts made by parliament in pursuance of the provisions of article 321.

All proposals for framing/amending recruitment rules are examined keeping in view the cadre structure of the organization and the circulars issued by the Govt. from time to time. After approval, the commission's advice in the matter is communicated to the Minister/Department concerned. More than 14000 Recruitment Rules have been framed/ amended so far.

DISCIPLINARY MATTERS

Under article 320 (3) of the constitution of commission are required to be consulted on the quantum of penalties in disciplinary cases affecting a person serving under the Government of India in a civil capacity.

EXTENSIION OF FUNCTIONS TO LOCAL BODIES ETC

Article 321 also employees the parliament to extend the functions of the public service commission to any local authority or other body corporate constituted by Law or by any public institutions.

RECRUITMENT & CONDITIONS OF SERVICE ETC

The provisions as contained in Article 309 & Article 311 of the constitution are also required to be read in conjunction with the provisions as contained in Article 320 of the constitution.

Union Public Service Commission :

Other than civil services and other organized services, UPSC advertises for different posts in Daily news papers (Saturdays) and in employment news/ Rozgar Samachar. The posts include recruitments for Union Territories where Public Service Commissions do not exist.

N.B: for such posts in the event of number of applications being large, commission will resort to short listing criteria to restrict number of candidates to be called for interview to a reasonable limit.

(a) On the basis of either qualifications and experience higher than the minimum prescribed for the post.
(b) On the basis of experience in the relevant fields.
(c) By counting experience before or after the acquisition of essential qualifications.
(d) By holding a screening test.

The candidates should therefore mention all the qualifications and experience in the relevant field over and above the minimum qualification and should attach attested/ self certified copies of the certificates in support there of.

Candidates called for interview will be reimbursed II class mail rail fare to & fro by the shortest route to the place of interview.

1.a. Indian Civil Services

UPSC Conducts Exams for various posts in central government. UPSC gives prescribed syllabus for various competitive examinations conducted by them. Indian Civil services Examination is conducted by UPSC for the following posts:-

(i) Indian Administrative Service I.A.S.
(ii) Indian foreign service. I.F.S.
(iii) Indian Police Service. I.P.S.
(iv) Indian P & T Accounts & Finance Service, Group “A”.

(v) Indian Audit and accounts service, Group "A"
(vi) Indian customs and central excise services group "A"
(vii) Indian Defense accounts service, Group "A"
(viii) Indian Revenue Service Group "A".
(ix) Indian ordnance factories service, Group A (Assistant works manager Non-technical)
(x) Indian Postal Service, Group "A"
(xi) Indian Civil Accounts Service, Group "A"
(xii) Indian Railway Traffic service, Group "A"
(xiii) Indian Railway Accounts Service, Group "A"
(xiv) Indian Railway personnel service, Group "A"
(xv) Posts of assistant security officer, Group "A" in Railway Protection Force.
(xvi) Indian Defense Estates Service, Group "A".
(xvii) Indian information service (Junior Grade) Group "A"
(xviii) Indian Trade Services Group "A" Grade III
(xix) Armed Forces Headquarters Civil Service, Group "B" (section officer's grade)
(xx) The Delhi, Andaman and Nicobar Islands, Laksha dweep, Daman & Diu and Dadra & Nagar Haveli Police Service, Group "B"

(*** All the above services have the same syllabus and same selection pattern. Services of the above are allotted to the successful candidates based on their RANK in the FINAL RESULT of CIVIL SERVICES EXAM and their service preference given in the MAIN APPLICATION)

PRELIMINARY

Changes in syllabus and pattern of the Preliminary Examination from 2011 in the scheme of Civil Services Examination

- As per the decision of Government of India, there shall be change in the syllabus and pattern of the Preliminary Examination from 2011 in the scheme of the Civil Services Examination.
- The Preliminary Examination shall now comprise of two compulsory Papers of 200 marks each and of two hours duration each. Detailed below is the new syllabus and pattern of the Preliminary Examination, which is brought to the notice of the prospective candidates intending to appear at the Civil Services Examination (CSE) in 2011 onwards:

Paper I - (200 marks) Duration: Two hours

- Current events of national and international importance

- History of India and Indian National Movement
- Indian and World Geography - Physical, Social, Economic geography of India and the World.
- Indian Polity and Governance – Constitution, Political System, Panchayati Raj, Public Policy, Rights Issues, etc.
- Economic and Social Development – Sustainable Development, Poverty, Inclusion, Demographics, Social Sector Initiatives, etc.
- General issues on Environmental ecology, Bio-diversity and Climate Change - that do not require subject specialization
- General Science.

Paper II- (200 marks) Duration: Two hours

- Comprehension
- Interpersonal skills including communication skills;
- Logical reasoning and analytical ability
- Decision making and problem solving
- General mental ability
- Basic numeracy (numbers and their relations, orders of magnitude etc.) (Class X level), Data interpretation (charts, graphs, tables, data sufficiency etc. -Class X level)
- English Language Comprehension skills (Class X level).
- Questions relating to English Language Comprehension skills of Class X level (last item in the Syllabus of Paper-II) will be tested through passages from English language only without providing Hindi translation thereof in the question paper.
- The questions will be of multiple choices, objective type.

A set of sample questions for both Papers is available on the UPSC website http://www.upsc.gov.in for reference of the prospective candidates.

The prospective candidates are advised to note that no changes are being introduced at this stage in the Civil Services (Main) Examination and Personality Test in the scheme of Civil Services Examination (CSE).

1.b. Indian Civil Services Syllabus For mains exams: (IAS Syllabus Mains)

General Studies

- Essay
- Compulsory English and Indian Language
- Agriculture
- Animal Husbandry and Veterinary Science
- Anthropology
- Botany

- Chemistry
- Civil Engineering
- Commerce and Accountancy
- Economics
- Electrical Engineering
- Geography
- Geology
- History
- Law
- Management
- Mathematics
- Mechanical Engineering
- Medical Science
- Philosophy
- Physics
- Political Science and International Relations
- Psychology
- Public Administration
- Sociology
- Statistics
- Zoology
- Arabic
- Assamese
- Bengali
- Chinese
- English
- French
- German
- Gujarati
- Hindi
- Kannada
- Kashmiri
- Konkani
- Malayalam
- Manipuri
- Marathi
- Nepali
- Oriya
- Pali
- Persian
- Punjabi
- Russian
- Sanskrit
- Sindhi
- Tamil
- Telugu
- Urdu
- Bodo
- Maithili
- Santali

General Guidelines

The nature and standard of questions in the General Studies papers will be such that a well-educated person will be able to answer them without any specialized study. The questions will be such as to test a candidate's general awareness of a variety of subjects, which will have relevance for a career in Civil Services. The questions are likely to test the candidate's basic understanding of all relevant issues, and ability to analyze, and take a view on conflicting socio-economic goals, objectives and demands. The candidates must give relevant, meaningful and succinct answers.

PAPER – I

1. **History of Modern India and Indian Culture**

   The History of Modern India will cover history of the country from about the middle of nineteenth century and would also include questions on important personalities who shaped the freedom movement and social reforms. The part relating to Indian culture will cover all aspects of Indian culture from the ancient to modern time as well as principal features of literature, arts and architecture.

2. **Geography of India**
   In this part, questions will be on the physical, economic and social geography of India.
3. **Constitution of India and Indian Polity**
   The part will include questions on the Constitution of India as well as all constitutional, legal, administrative and other issues emerging from the politico-administrative system prevalent in the country.
4. **Current National Issues and Topics of Social Relevance**
   This part is intended to test the candidates' awareness of current national issues and topics of social relevance in present-day India, such as the following.
   (i) The Indian economy and issues relating to planning, mobilization of resources, growth, development and employment.
   (ii) Issues arising from the social and economic exclusion of large sections from the benefits of development.
   (iii) Other issues relating to the development and management of human resource.
   (iv) Health issues including the management of Public Health, Health education and ethical concerns regarding health-care, medical research and pharmaceuticals.
   (v) Law enforcement, internal security and related issues such as the preservation of communal harmony.
   (vi) Issues relating to good governance and accountability to the citizens including the maintenance of human rights, and of probity in public life.
   (vii) Environmental issues, ecological preservation, conservation of natural resources and national heritage.

General Studies Syllabus Paper II

1. India and the World
   This part will include questions to test candidate's awareness of India's relationship with the world in various spheres such as the following.
   Foreign Affairs with special emphasis on India's relations of neighboring countries and in the region.
   Security and defense related matters.

Nuclear policy, issues and conflicts.
The Indian Diaspora and its contribution to the world.

2. India's Economic Interaction with the World
In this part, questions will be on economic and trade issues such as foreign trade, foreign investment, economic and diplomacy issues relating to oil, gas and energy flows; the role and functions of I.M.F. World Bank, W.T.O. WIPO etc. which influence India's economic interaction with other countries and international institutions.

3. Developments in the field of Science and Technology, IT and space.
In this part, questions will test the candidate's awareness of the developments in the field of science and technology, information technology and space.

4. International Affairs and Institutions
This part will include questions on important events in world affairs and on international institutions.

5. Statistical analysis, graphs and diagrams
This part will test the candidate's ability to draw conclusions from information presented in statistical, graphical or diagrammatical form and to interpret them.

Civil Services

The examination pattern in civil service is two tier system.
Preliminaries (Prelims) - New system from 2011onwards :
Paper I : 200 Marks - 2 hrs duration
Paper II : 200 Marks - 2 hrs duration
After qualifying in prelims one has to write mains

Mains : Paper I General Studies – 300m Marks
Optional I 300 Marks
Optional II 300 Marks
Essay writing 300 Marks
General English 150 Marks
Total 1350 Marks

The successful candidates in Mains are invited for personal interviews

Personal interview : 300 Marks
Age Limit : 21 - 30 years
Four attempts for general candidates (prelims)
Seven attempts for OBC, SC, ST candidates.

Importance for Regional Languages

With medium of instructions in regional languages by recognized universities, the candidates are not conversant with English/ Hindi. To help the candidates, UPSC has introduced optionals in regional languages. In the personal interviews also to make the candidates comfortable in replies, system of interpretation was introduced. Telugu, Tamil, Kannada, Malayalam and other regional language experts assist the personal interview board in interpretation. The questions of the members of the interview board are translated into candidate's language. The replies of the candidate are interpreted for the benefit of the member. It gives a level playing field for the candidate. He will not be deprived of his handicap with English language.

Indian Forest Services

This is meant of recruitment in Forest Services, This is an All India Examination. The training after selection is given at Dehradun. They are posted as divisional Forest Officer / District Forest Officers they can raise up to Principal Chief conservator of Forests of the state cadre which they are allotted. It comes under Ministry of environment and forests.

Indian Economic Serviee / Indian Statistical Service

This is meant for specialized jobs in Economics and statistics departments. Economics and Statistics Post Graduates compete for these jobs. The examinations are conducted in the month of November for 3 days. The results are announced and personal interviews held in May. The successful candidates in exams have to fill up detailed application form (DAF) supplied by the commission and send it to the commission. After the personal interview the list of selected candidates is notified. For the year 2009 for IES personal interviews 39 candidates are selected. For Indian statistics service 26 candidates are selected.

Indian Engineering Services

UPSC annually conducts engineering service entrance exams in the month of June for All India Engineering Services. Based on the results of exams candidates are interviewed in Feb – March and the results announced in May in order of merit. During 2009 the following number of candidates are selected :

1.	Civil Engineering Group		-	205	Reserve	64
2.	Mechanical	,,	-	130	,,	40
3.	Electrical	,,	-	59	,,	26

4. Electronics and Telecom	,,	-	75	,,	08
Total		-	469		138

This is an All India competitive examination meant for recruitment of Engineers in various wings of Central Govt. The departments include – Railways, Telecommunications, CPWD, (central public works department) CCW (civil construction wing) Prasara Bharati (Doordarshan and All India Radio).

Toppers in 2009

1. Civil Engineering Group		-	Mr. Pridhvi Raj Panigrahi
2. Mechanical	,,	-	Mr. Amit Joshi
3. Electrical	,,	-	Mr. Akash Sharma
4. Electronics and Telecom	,,	-	Mr. Vaibhav Agarwal

Geologists Examination

The examinations for recruitment of Geologists at National level are conducted in December every year. Personality interviews are held in September the following year. The appointments are announced in November. For the exams conducted in 2008 the following no. of candidates were selected in 2009.

	General	*OBC*	*SC*	*ST*	*Total*
(1) Geologists (Junior) Group A Category – I	109	55	29	16	209
(2) Junior Hydro Geologist (Scientist– B) Group A & Asst Hydrologists Group B Category – II	06	02	01	01	10

Results of 2008 – Appointment for List I - 215 candidates (Geologists).

Appointment for List II – 36 candidates (Hydro Geologists)

Combined Medical Service Examination

UPSC conducts written test for combined medical services in the month of January every year. The Gazette notification is issued every year in the month of September. Detailed application form containing

rules for combined medical service (CMS) and summary sheet are available at **http://www.USPC.Gov.in.** The results are announced in the month of May. This is the test for doctors in various central organizations. Candidate has to learn more about different organizations, specialties.
UPSC:

Indian Navy

Youth can aspire to become Short service commissioned officers. Applications are invited at regular intervals from unmarried male and female candidates. The eligibility conditions are :

- Age – 19 ½ to 25 yrs.
- Educational qualification: First class Degree with minimum of 60% aggregate marks from a recognized university.
  (Candidates appearing for exams need not apply)
- Physical standards : Height AND Weight
  Male 157 & Female 152 Cms with correlated weight
- Eye sight 6/36

Selection Process

Candidates will be issued call up for service selection board (SSB) interviews based on their performance in educational qualifications. SSB interviews for short listed candidates will be scheduled during Jan – June at Bangalore, Bhopal or Coimbatore. The SSB interview is conducted over 5 days in two stages.

Stage I – Intelligence Test, Picture preparation Test and Group Discussion. (One day).
Stage II - Psychological Tests, Group test and personal interview (4 days).
Stage III - Special Medical Examination

Candidates selected and declared medically fit will be appointed for training in order of all India merit depending on number of vacancies.

Training commences in July. Candidates will be inducted as officers in the rank of sub -lieutenant and undergo naval orientation course at the **Indian naval academy, Ezhimala,** Kerala followed by professional training at various naval training establishments/ units / ships. They will be on probation for 2 years. Only unmarried candidates are eligible to undergo training. On successful completion of training he/she will be commissioned as sub – lieutenant.

Indian Navy – Short Service Commissioned Officers

(1) Recruitments are done on yearly basis. Course commences in July. Short Service Commission is granted for Ten years, extendable for 14 years.

(2) Indian Navy recruits candidates for Permanent Commissioned Officers in different wings in January.

Indian Air Force

Indian Air Force invites applications from unmarried male Indian citizens for selections test in August to join as Air men in Group (Y) – Non Technical.

The recruitment test is not for selection as Officers/ Pilots/ Navigators.

Educational Qualifications	:	Passed Intermediate (10+2) with Science / Arts/ Commerce Subjects with 50% marks.
Age	:	16 to 20 yrs by January.
Tenure and Training	:	Initial period of 20 yrs extendable up to 57 yrs. Joint basic phase training = 12 weeks.
Written Test	:	August.
Personal Interview	:	After Medical Test.

Staff Selection Commissions

Ministry of Personnel, Public grievances and pensions, Department of personnel and training has set up Staff selection commissions (SSC) at different regions – Northern, Southern, Eastern, Western etc. for recruitment of Group C employees. They include Accountant, Upper Division clerks, lower division clerks, stenographers, Junior Hindi Translators etc.

The SSC conducts examinations for screening and interviews are conducted. Selected candidates will be nominated to different departments. All Govt. offices place their requirements before SSC and based on the requisitions, SSC advertises in Employment news & Local news papers for the posts.

Railway Recruitment Board (RRB)

Ministry of Railways has setup different RRBs in different railway zones. Besides individual recruitments by RRB, centralized employment notice is also given for certain posts - Technician signal Gr II, Technician signal Gr III, Telecom maintainer Grade III, wireless telecom maintainer Gr. III etc.

Centralized employment notice of Railway Recruitment Boards include – Stenographer, Law Asst, Finger Print examiner, Senior publicity inspector, catering manager, Asst. Master (PG teachers male and female). Trained graduate teachers, English lecturers, Primary Railway teacher, P.G. Teacher in different subjects, physical training instructor, craft teacher etc.

Different RRBs

RRB Ahmedabad, Ajmer, Allahabad, Bangalore, Bhopal, Bhuvaneswar, Bilaspur, Chandigarh, Chennai, Ghorakpur, Guwhati, Jammu, Sri Nagar, Kolkata, Malda, Mumbai, Muzaffarpur, Patna, Ranchi, Secundrabad and Trivandram.

State Public Service Commissions

Each state has a Public Service Commission appointed statutorily under constitutional provisions. The state PSCs recruit persons for Group I, Group II, Group III posts of the concerned states. Recruitment for union territories like Chandigarh, Andaman & Nicobar Islands etc. is done by UPSC.

Group I Services

Most prestigious posts in the states are covered under these services. Revenue Divisional Officer, Divisional Police Officers, Commercial Tax officers, Panchayat Officer, Labour Officers, Survey and Land Records, Excise etc services come under Group I.

Examinations are conducted to screen the candidates. It is not a regular annual examination as in the case of UPSC. Each state depending on the requirement advertise for the posts. Heavy demand is there for such recruits. These young recruits in Revenue and Police after completion of about 10-15 yrs of service in the state get promotions / conferment into IAS & IPS cadres. They are known as departmental promotees. Ratio of promotees Vs Direct recruits is also prescribed for each state. Cadre wise posts are notified for each state. A total of about 5159 officers of IAS work in different states.

Candidates appearing for State service commission have to know about the job requirements and the organizational structure. Demand for Revenue, Police, Commercial Taxes, and Excise is increasing day by day since they are largely connected with the public. Besides service motto, authority, power and money are involved in these posts.

The recruiting agencies at times succumb to pressures at state level and scams are unearthed in some States. Candidates shall not fall prey to such middlemen and practice immoral methods to get through the selection process.

Hard work, study, integrity are required. Maintain them. Corruption is to be avoided at all levels. It is easy to preach but difficult to practice. From the beginning start the career with morals. You may not end up in problems/troubles.

Advertisement for Group I services of different Sate Public Service Commissions appear occasionally. The system of selection is on the lines of U.P.S.C. Andhra Pradesh Public Service commission Group I Service examinations are taken as an example. The preparation part is important in all the examinations. Competition for this exam is very heavy. So candidate has to prepare in a systematic manner. At least 100 days preparation is required. Plan to win Group I preliminary is given:

Paper I : Essay : Marks 150 : 3 Hrs duration

20 to 25 questions are expected in Geography.

Subject matter should be at your finger tips to get score in Geography. Current topics and standard points are mixed together 1/6th of the time is to be spared for Geography. A person with good reading habits of 8 to 9 hours per day shall allot 140 hours (out of 100 days). Ordinary person has to spare 160 hours.

Reading tips

Detailed study of Atlas. Candidate should be able to answer easily. (Lakes, river flowing areas). While reading, comparative study with current trends is to be done. Combine economy with Geography, particularly in respect of Agriculture, Industry, Transport wings. Divide the subjects into three parts: World Geography, Indian Geography and State Geography. 40 % of time for Indian Geography and 20% for State Geography is to be given.

Paper II. History - Polity : 150 Marks : 3Hrs duration

25 questions are expected. Daily 2 ½ hours preparation is needed. Keeping in mind Prelims and Mains objective type reading is suggested. Important dates which have changed the history are to be remembered.

Division of Subjects	:	Ancient and middle age history, state history modern Indian history.
Important	:	For Arts student preparation is comparatively easy.

Ref. Books : Be prepared for 100% answering.
NCERT Books
Ancient Indian History – R.S. Sharma
Medieval Indian History - Satish Chandra
Modern History – Bipin Chandra.

Polity :

10 to 15 questions are expected. Daily 2 hours reading is advised. Objective type for Prelims, analytical study for Mains are suggested.

Division of Subjects : Central Government, State Administration, Local Bodies, Supreme Court, High Courts and constitution.

Ref. Books : Indian Government – Politics
Indian Polity – Laxmi Kanth.

Paper III : Economy : Marks 150 : 3 Hrs duration

15 questions are expected. Minimum of 80 hours preparation. In Economy compared to concepts, facts are important.

Population, Density of population, literacy rate, male-female ratio, SC, ST population are to be studied.

Reference Books :

Indian Economy – Dutt and Sundaram
Economic survey – 2010 – 2011.
50 yrs of A.P. - M. Hanumanta Rao

Paper IV : Science and Technology : Marks 150 : 3 Hrs duration

20 to 25 questions. Minimum of 2 ½ of hours per day study is required. Contemporary changes in modern science and technology are important.

Ref. Books :

Science Reporter Magazine
Civils prelims previous papers.

Paper V : Data Interpretation and Problem Solving : 150 Marks duration 3 Hrs Questions will be in 3 sections

Ref. Book : A Modern Approach to Verbal Reasoning
R.S. Agarwal

Collegiate Service Commissions

Some of the states have constituted Collegiate Service Commissions for the recruitment of lectures in various departments. The notification is given occasionally. State Level Entrance Tests are conducted to screen the candidates. Successful candidates are interviewed depending on the number of vacancies available in each department - Regional languages, English, Hindi, Sanskrit, Urdu, Economics, Political Science, Commerce, Physical Sciences, Biological Sciences, Computers, Physical education, Library Sciences etc. The commission is headed by a Chairman and few members. Recruitment process is not regular, yearly based. At times there may not be any recruitment for 4 to 5 years. Presently very few states have such commissions.

Most of the unsuccessful candidates who aspire for Civil services or Group I service of the state wait for their turn to be recruited as lecturers. The University Grants Commission scales and Sate Govt. scales are optional to the lecturers. Under career advance programme (CAP) a lecturer after 12 yrs of service will automatically get Reader/Associate professor scale. Private colleges select separately.

Appointment by Universities

Each university has a set of rules to recruit lecturers/Associate Professor/ Professor by open notification. The vice-chancellor of the university appoints a committee to recruit the employers as per requirements of each department of the university. Recruitments for specialized posts with research experience will be conducted at regular intervals. Universities recognized by UGC have to follow the rules stipulated by UGC in the selection process. Vice – Chancellor will be the Chairman of the committee. Outside assessors as experts from other universities are invited to act as panelists/experts. Personal interview mainly deals with the research work done by the candidate. Papers published in national/ International Journals/ (guidance to research scholars) Books published/ Seminar papers will count. Since it is a teaching job and research oriented, subject specialist in the field assesses the candidate. Age relaxation, higher pay scale etc are at the discretion of the University authorities.

Personal interview has more weight age. Candidate can impress the committee with his commitment, sincerity and hard work. Normally the ratio of candidates applied/called for interview will be very less. No need for any screening test. The head of the department/ Dean/ UGC nominee and outside expert judge the competence of the candidate.

UGC scales for associate Professor's / Professors posts are very attractive. About Rs. 60-70 thousands are offered as initial start of the pay. It is a non transferable job. Scholars, educationists, researchers prefer to work in centers of higher excellence. However nepotism, caste based politics have entered the seats of learning. Political interference in the appointments has taken place. Candidates with high caliber may not be the only criteria for the selection. Try your Luck.

Part II Civil Services Examinations

Preparation for Civils

"It is difficult to succeed in Civils"

It is a common syndrome – and opinion of many a competitors. It is only a misconception. Hard work and dedication are important. Most of the time the candidate collects lot of material available on the subject. But he fails to understand what UPSC expects from them. With out proper understanding there is no use in collecting information. He will not be in a position to read it and keep it in a proper method for digestion. They worry mostly about the material which they do not read. Better take the advise of seniors, friends and lecturers. Select good books. Constant reading, understanding what is read, communication skills (written and oral) are important. Knowledge of the subject helps in preliminaries and effective communication helps in personal interview and can gain command over the subject.

Allot More Time for Optionals

Daily 15 hours study is suggested. Since more number of marks are allotted for optionals, 60% time is to be allotted for them. Rest of the time can be allotted for General studies. If the preliminary optional is selected for main optional also preparation will be easy. Have a thorough study on the different concepts in the syllabus. Follow your own methodology to study and memorize. To get more marks in General studies one has to read standard books two to three times. Have a time frame accordingly. Allot time slots for revision also.

In the Prelims General studies, current affairs is vital. Reading of news papers will help. Analyze yourself which is good or bad. While reading the news, frame questions in your mind. The main concept of optional is to be studied minimum 10 times for total understanding. Read the previous question papers so that you can have a thorough knowledge. When you complete preparation for optionals practice many number of model papers with in the time frame of UPSC exams. It gives an idea to analyze your strengths and weakness, as well as speed in writing.

Selection of optionals is also vital. Based on individual aptitude and information available, they are to be chosen. When you choose optionals at least two years preparation is needed. Do not get bored. Love the subject. **Civils preparation is like a marathon race. To win over one shall have dedication, love in doing things and patience.**

Suggestions

1. Make it a habit to read quickly - 12 to 15 pages in an hour.
2. If you can answer 85 to 90 question in prelims General Studies, you are sure to win. Try this line.
3. Do not get disheartened. There are people who did not succeed even after 5 yrs preparation.
4. Do not loose hopes if you fail in first attempt.
5. Have complete knowledge about the various Government committees and reports submitted by them.
6. Get relaxed when you feel fatigue.

These are only tips. Have your own method to prepare.

Good Luck.

Books/Journals to Read

While preparing for the examinations for jobs and personal interviews it is your choice to read different books and journals. It depends upon the resources you have and the library facilities you have in your Town/City/Office. General Knowledge books are plenty in market. Manorama year books and India 2010 [published yearly by publication division] have lot of information. Lot of career oriented Magazines besides Employment news in English and Rozgar samachar in Hindi and Yojana [published by Publications Divisions, of Govt of India in English, Hindi, Telugu and other languages] are available. The issues contain lot of material useful for candidates appearing for competitive examinations.

Maintain a Note Book

Take a note book of 200 to 300 pages. Allot 10 pages for each section and go on jotting down notes on different subjects.

Chapters can be

1. Current topics.
2. Parliament.
3. International Matters
4. Literature (Regional)

5. Science and Technology.
6. Subject oriented matters.
7. National Awards.
8. National Sports and Games.
9. Governors of different states.
10. Central Ministers and so on.

Minimum time you have to prepare vigioursly is 3 months (90 days). During the period read important national dailies in English/ Hindi/ Regional language and go on updating the information. Salient points are to be noted down. On 31st of December of every year chronology of events will be published. Keep a copy of it for reference.

Editorials

Make it a habit to read Editorials of main English dailies - Hindu / New Indian Express / Times of India / Hindustan Times etc. Note down the major points discussed in the editorial. Similarly in the edit page, articles by eminent writers appear in different issues. They include articles by Mr. Inder Malhotra, Prem Bhatia, B.G. Vergheese etc. Keep a watch on Sunday special articles. Reading is a habit. Depending upon your taste you can cultivate assimilating the information.

Listening to Radio

With the advent of hundreds of channels on TV, All India Radio has become out dated. But the programmes like spotlight broadcast at 9.15pm every day by Delhi Station of All India Radio at national level, contain discussion of current topics. At 9.30 pm on Sunday current affairs is broadcast. Listen to them to update your knowledge. Copies of the broadcasts are available at All India Radio. Obtain them if possible.

Journals

Weeklies and fortnightlies dealing with political matters publish items on current topics. Have a detailed note on the issues and jot down in your note book for ready reference before going to the examination Hall/personal interview. Let us take an example.

Women's Reservation Bill in Parliament :

- History of the introduction of the Bill by different Govts.
- Stand of different political parties.
- Passing of the bill in Lokha Sabha in March 2010.
- Future of the Bill.
- Pros and cons.
- Difficulties if any.

Similarly you can list out 10 to 15 current topics and note down the opinion of senior editors/ seasoned politicians/ leaders in parliament. While replying the question in Examination or personal interview the opinion of eminent personalities if quoted, is well taken. Avoid controversies and severe criticism on Govt. Be prepared to answer the typical question – what is your personal opinion?

The answer should be:

(a) Clear cut opinion on the subject.
(b) So and so has objected / accepted. I agree with him / I don't agree.
(c) I have no idea. (it is a very bad reply)
(d) Historical perspective.
(e) Persons mainly associated with the subject.
(f) Public Opinion.

Cultivate Writing Habit

During the preparations make it a point to have a drill of writing **mock examinations at your leisure time**. It gives confidence, speed, thinking power, thought process, time consciousness. Start the exercise. On a particular Sunday have a good breakfast. Take the previous year question paper. Sit down tightly at the desk at 9 am. Keep watching your pace of answering. Time allotted is Three Hours. Phase out time for all the questions. Go on writing as if you are in the examination hall. Don't verify books. Do the exercise once a month to know your weakness. Check list–

1. Verify the replies later. Find out the discrepancies by your self.
2. Time allotted is 180minutes. Last question also shall have at least 10minutes time. So speed up.
3. Give sub headings, and Main Headings.
4. Give inotiations statistics and facts.

Examination Hall - Points to Remember

Spend first 3 minutes to go through the question paper. Many candidates do not turn the question paper and watch second page. They observe it when they come out of the examination hall.

- Read all the instructions at the top – time given, compulsory questions, choice given. Select your choice questions.
- Instructions to be followed. Hall Ticket number to be written.
- Give page number for answer sheets.
- Objective type questions - ABCD tick marks. Be careful.
- Put question number properly on the answer sheet.
- Read the question carefully. Find out the implications in the question.

- Think for a while before start answering.
- Start Answering.
- Watch the time.
- For 3hr duration – [5 questions.] Answer each question in 30 to 35 min.
- Avoid last minute answering.
- Go through the answers at the end for 2 to 3 minutes.
- Add last minute ideas at the bottom.
- Visible hand writing.
- Paragraph division and subheading.
- Add Quotations / Facts and Figures.
- Page numbering of answer sheets.
- Avoid repetition of same matter in the subsequent answers.
- Don't write what all you know.
- Write whatever is needed.
- Do not pose yourself as if you know everything.
- Do not give statistics unnecessarily.
- Use colour pens to highlight.

Among the essay questions write the first question which you feel confident. Don't write answers for the last two questions in a hurry. During the valuation your mediocre knowledge will be noticed. Answers for 20 marks questions shall contain 4 pages of A4 size. All the 4 pages shall have sub headings, main headings. Example: Causes for French revolution :

1. Political 2. Religious 3. Social 4. Economic causes. Each one is to be written in a separate page.

These points may appear childish at your age. But keep a watch on all the points to be sure of your success in the examination.

Comparative Grading

Answering all the questions well is not the criteria. The following points will be judged during evaluation by examiners

- Comparative Grading / Highest score.

  If the candidates are say 250

  Persons required for selection : 4

  Persons called for interview: 1 : 6 ratio : 6x4=24.

So among the 250 candidates, persons with highest score will be called for personal interviews. If total marks are 100. Those who obtained 85 and below up to 24th Rank will be selected for interview. In this scenario candidate has to impress the evaluators in such a way that his way of answering is the best.

Criteria :

- Best presentation
- Analytical approach.
- Reasoning.
- Arguments on both sides.
- Good Beginning.
- Neat closing Remarks.
- Quotable quotes.
- Facts & Figures
- Legible hand writing.
- Approach to the subject.
- Knowledge about the subject
- References quoted.
- Scientific thinking.
- Minute details.

While valuing the answers, marks will be awarded depending on the way of presentation. The candidate is judged by his answers. No direct contact is there between the candidate and examiner. Normal practice is they will not go through word by word, sentence by sentence. The total approach is taken into consideration, for essay questions and paragraph questions.

Think for a while before you ink.

4

Interview Preparation

"Someone who can articulate vision clearly and someone with energy and should be able to energize others" – Jack Welch, CEO, General Electric on qualities that he looks for in a candidate

Interview Preparation

At Infosys, at most care is taken to ensure their main entrance gates are clean and tidy. Weekly checks are done to monitor the same. It is important to understand why such importance is awarded to something as basic as the entry points. According to the Infosys management, Infosys entry points are the first touch points for the customers, partners, suppliers and prospects visiting their campuses. Hence, forming the right first impression takes centre stage. Similarly, résumé is the first step in the long, daunting task of finding a job and we want you to share similar thought about the same.

ZERO Size Résumé

ZERO size is the new fashion statement. Female actors in the movie industry are going gaga over ZERO size. ZERO size represents slim and trim. You need to remember that résumé is not your auto-biography. Résumés also have gone slim from 4-5 page résumés to 1 page résumé. Writing long, elaborate résumés are a thing of the past. Today employers/ HR personnel don't have time to read long résumés. Large companies like Accenture, Infosys, Microsoft browse through more than a 1000 résumés to shortlist 1 candidate for job offer. Considering most of these companies run with skeletal thin HR teams there is very high likelihood they don't have the time to browse through all résumés. Hence, writing a crisp and short "ZERO Size" résumé is very important. In this chapter, we try and help you distil your experience into what we call KISS (Keep It Short and Salesy) approach. Anything more than a page is a BIG NO in a world that has moved from Test Cricket to T20.

> **Did you know?**
> Résumés on an average get about **15-20 seconds** attention time

Anatomy of Résumé

Consider résumé like a self-advertisement. Think of yourself as the product you would be selling through this advertisement. While you don't need to oversell, you need to capture all the USPs (Unique Selling Points) about yourself in the résumé. Advertising as we all know is not a science. It is an art and here in this book we will help you master that art. It is all about branding yourself for a rewarding corporate career. You should use the résumé as a way of differentiating yourself from the JANATA (CROWD). Employers need to feel compelled and attracted to call you for an interview looking at your résumé.

Heading

This section of the résumé should cover your first name and last name, address and contact details. With social networking sites like Linked In, Face book becoming popular there are multiple ways in which you can be contacted but you should avoid providing all the detail and stick to providing a contact number where you can be easily reached. You can provide the office desk number, if you are working and your company provides DID (direct inward dialing) facility and the call doesn't land with the receptionist. Since, you are normally contacted during business hours, it is suggested to provide mobile number and personal e-mail ID. You should also add a scanned passport photograph in the heading. Your need to find a job is much higher than the employer's need to find you. So, it is very important to be easily accessible to the prospective employers/ HR managers.

> **Did you Know?**
> **Amitabh Bachchan** known for his rich and stellar voice was rejected by **All India Radio** when auditioned. He later went on to become the super star of Indian Bollywood

Objective

This section needs at most care when writing the résumé. It is better to drop this section from the résumé if you are not clear about what specific job you are applying. A good objective is a way of telling the prospective employer your goals. We encourage using buzzwords and motherhood statements here ONLY when you are comfortable to deal with questions that might come up during the course of interview. Avoid "**copy paste**" objectives from sample résumés listed either in this book or elsewhere. How many of us have not used something like below while creating our résumé for our first job

"Exciting work in a passionate company that will provide ample opportunities to learn and grow in my career"

Experience

This section forms the heart of your résumé. For those who are applying for their first job you can always use the project experience from your Engineering/MCA. Experience should always be listed in reverse chronological order. Most recent experience should be listed first and then previous experiences. Experience should include the duration, title, role in the organization/project, size of the organization/project, name of your employer, city/country and accomplishments.

> **Did you know?**
>
> **Winston Churchill** failed the military written exam twice. He later went on to become one of the best leaders of the world

> **FUN TIME!!!**Interviewer: You have listed Oracle as your area of expertise. Please take us through your experience working on Oracle
>
> Interviewee: Oh....Is that in my résumé? Aaahhh... Can I have a look at it?
>
> **MORAL**: Know every inch of your résumé. Feigning ignorance about facts stated in YOUR résumé puts a question mark on your honesty and credibility

Education/Certifications

This is the next most important element of the résumé after experience and hence should appear after your experience. A lot of companies give importance to education background. Companies like

Infosys would like to see distinction and above percentages (75%) all the way from secondary class (10th). While some IT companies only hire Engineers or MCAs for their Software development division. Hence, it is very important to capture the right amount of detail. You should specify the board/university, year of completion, percentage/grade, and Special subjects. Committee also encourages you to club your certifications in the same section. Certifications like project management (PMI) or technical (Oracle, Sun, Microsoft) or any others should be captured under the same heading.

Achievements

This is the last section of your résumé and should have all the punch to attract the attention. You can talk about any publications, speaker ship, and any prizes won in sports in this section. For instance, papers/ articles in magazines, journals, conferences should be listed here. You should also specify the conferences at which you have presented your paper. You should also capture the awards you have received in this section. Awards at company level or by external agencies provide the right ammunition to your résumé.

FUNTIME!!!

Interviewer: Tell us about your achievements

Interviewee: I have got double promotion when I was in class 3 to class 5

MORAL: You should avoid quoting examples that are irrelevant or too old for someone to appreciate what you are saying

References

References give credibility to your résumé. You should include references of your boss in previous/current organization, customer you worked with, HR head OR executive management staff in your previous/ current company. References need not be included in the résumé to save space and restrict the résumé to 1 page. You can either say "References available on request".

Did you know?

Beethoven was considered "hopeless" at composing music by his teacher. Rest is history

Others

You should avoid mentioning your salary details or your expectation from the new job in the résumé. You can always keep this for a face to face discussion later. If the job AD you are applying for has clearly asked you to mention salary details then you don't have a choice. Even then you can always make a brief mention in your cover letter.

101 WORDS TO "USE" IN YOUR RÉSUMÉ

Abolished	Accepted
Adhered	Advised
Aided	Appointed
Approved	Appraised
Administered	Assembled
Analyzed	Arranged
Adjudged	Acclaimed
Bid	Boosted
Billed	Built
Bridged	Coded
Carried out	Channeled
Collected	Circumvented
Communicated	Compiled
Completed	Conducted
Contacted	Contracted
Coordinated	Counseled
Created	Captured
Commenced	Delegated
Detailed	Designed
Determined	Developed
Directed	Dispatched
Distributed	Documented
Disseminate	Delivered
Edited	Established
Expended	Experienced
Envisioned	Enlightened
Functioned	Factored
Formed	Fulfilled
Generated	Groomed
Gathered	Greatest
Handled	Hired

Implemented	Incorporated
Improved	Inspected
Interviewed	Introduced
Invented	Innovated
Maintained	Managed
Met	Motivated
Measured	Monitored
Negotiated	Operated
Orchestrated	Ordered
Organized	Oversaw
Performed	Planned
Prepared	Presented
Produced	Programmed
Published	Purchased
Recommended	Recorded
Reduced	Referred
Represented	Researched
Reviewed	Saved
Screened	Served as
Served on	Sold
Suggested	Supervised
Solutionized	Showed
Taught	Tested
Trained	Typed
Tracked	Terminated
Tailored	Value Added
Wrote	Worked

Technology Advances

Company website

Most of the large organizations ask you to create/upload your résumé on their website as they receive thousands of résumés in response to job AD and hence becomes impossible for them to manually scan through all of them. Once they get saved to their database, the use résumé scanners to filter through the résumés. In this case you have the advantage of browsing through the company site to find out more details like job description, about the company and interacting with their HR personnel (through email id). The information gathered should be used effectively in your résumé.

Job portals

There are a good number of job portals on the internet like Naukri, Monster, Times Jobs etc. For senior management positions in the IT industry these portals are very ineffective and result in getting job opening emails for anything and everything based on what the job portal scanner has found as fit for you. Look for job description or gather more information about the opening, company and environment through business magazines and accordingly use the right keywords in your résumé

Social Networking

In the last few years, social networking sites like LinkedIN and Facebook have gained a lot of prominence and have become an important source for employers. Having a good profile, recommendations and a large network on these sites always helps.

Electronic Format

When you store your résumé on any of the above sites, it gets stored as text into their database and hence might lose formatting or in some cases images. Employers then use search engines to look for keywords (refer to the list on the top). What it means is that all your fancy formatting will go for a toss. So, following the below guidelines help :

1. Avoid images – Unless the website provides an option
2. Avoid bold, italicizing, tabular formats and lines
3. Avoid using non-standard fonts

This can kill all the effort you have put into creating a great résumé. So, we suggest you to convert your résumé to text format before uploading and see for yourself once.

Did you know?

The difference between CV (Curriculum Vitae) and Résumé. CV is detailed and runs 4 or more pages. It carries more detail about your professional experience or educational background.

TIPS

1. UPDATED means OUTDATED

In the rush of the moment to find a new job, you might take the old copy of your résumé and start adding new projects/experience. By doing this you create longer version of the résumé and also tend to lose out some irrelevant content in the résumé or highlight those skills/experience that are currently not your core skills.

2. Give your résumé a FACIAL

Sanjay and Kamesh are two employees working in an organization in the same division with similar experience and similar skills. Sanjay is an exceptional performer while Kamesh is average in his performance. Sanjay doesn't spend enough time on his résumé while Kamesh creates a nicely crafted, elegant looking résumé. Which résumé do you think is going to get selected in screening process? The answer is "No brainer".

3. Copying is Lethal

Don't take the résumé of a successful person and copy it. Résumé is an exercise of self-introspection to find out your strengths, weaknesses and achievements. Hence, what applies to someone else doesn't apply to you.

CASE STUDY

Smitha Murthy is looking for a change and finds this Ad in the local newspaper. Smitha reads the advertisement.

INFYPRO Advertisement
WE MISS YOU

INFYPRO is an IT company based out of Bangalore. INFYPRO was founded in 1995 and has offices in 100 countries across the globe. We have grown from a 100 member company in 1995 to 90,000 employees currently. Our revenues have grown from 10 Million USD to 50 Billion USD during the same period. INFYPRO is committed to innovation and R&D. The company spends 5% of its revenues in R&D every year. INFYPRO has 1000 patents to its credit and has another 50 patents pending approval. Our products are known for their quality. Analysts have rated INFYPRO as the leader in ERP application space continuously for the last 5 years. INFYPRO's products also have received technology excellence awards by independent bodies/ associations.

We are looking for experienced product development managers working as part of our R&D division. In this role, you will be responsible for the management of product deliverables, support and quality of the product.

You should demonstrate a successful track record of managing products, ability to innovate and work independently. You should be a graduate on computer sciences and minimum experience of 15 years in product development. ERP product development experience preferred. Technology background should be Java/CPP

If you meet this requirement, please send your CV to jobs@INFYPRO.com. You can also upload your résumés on http://www.INFYPRO.Com

Sanjay sinha
HR Manager
INFYPRO
14, Bannerghatta Road
Bengalooru
Ph: 080-22220000

Assessment

Smitha's assessment of the AD is as follows

INFYPRO is looking for a product development manager

1. Should be innovative and work independently
2. Role involves development and support
3. Experience of 15+ years
4. Graduate in computer sciences
5. Preferred: ERP application development experience

She also concludes that the role is part of their R&D division.

A deeper look also highlights the below

1. Innovation
2. Patents
3. Product quality and excellence
4. Fast paced growth
5. Competitive

Smitha then searches the company website www.INFYPRO.com and finds the below information

INFYPRO is owned by Indian business group that is also into other businesses like Retail, Manufacturing, Telecom and Financial Services. CEO of the company is based out of USA and has worked in the past with large multi-national companies. Company has 50% of its workforce in India.

Smitha then calls the HR Manager (Sanjay Sinha) and gathers the below information. Sanjay tells Smitha that the company is expanding their product development division and that they are going to add few more products very soon. They are looking for top-notch engineers who can help them design products that are ahead of competition.

Smitha then looks at her Linked IN contacts and finds an ex-colleague (Varun Sarma) who is currently with INFYPRO. Varun tells her that INFYPRO is growing at a fast pace and hence they need senior resources. Varun also tells her that the company is a true MNC and they believe in HIRE and FIRE policy. They believe in changing and changing fast to suit customer requirements. Employees who cannot adapt to the change are discarded. Varun told Smitha that salary is not a constraint for the right resource and that INFYPRO are pay masters.

Smitha then analyses what would be her key selling points and how she should she project herself in her résumé. She lists down the below key selling points

- Ten year product Development R & D experience with IBM and Microsoft.
- Three patents awarded and 2 filed with US PTO
- Managed Product development teams of size 100.
- Past of successful products like Ingres and ERwin
- Speaker at TECH – Days – Expo

DO IT YOURSELF

Go to any website like www.infosys.com and find out the job openings they have. Then find a job opening that closely matches that of your skill set. Try gathering more details about the role, company and environment and accordingly prepare your résumé

Sample Résumé 1

Rakesh Sharma

14 Club House • Mall Road, Simla • +91-1234567890 •
rakesh.sharma@example.com

- Reputed Pune University graduate offering a strong academic background in IT combined with excellent internship experience as a software engineer.
- Consistently recognized for technical troubleshooting skills used to rapidly and cost-effectively resolve challenging technical issues.
- Quickly learn and master new technology; equally successful in both team and self-directed settings; and proficient in a range of computer systems, languages, tools and testing methodologies.

Education

Pune UNIVERSITY – Pune, India, Degree expected 5/10

B.S. in Computer Information Systems program • GPA: 3.7/4.0

Concurrent Employment with College Studies:

- **Student Helpdesk Support** (2007 to Present): Provide networking/ desktop support and perform mainframe and account maintenance tasks. Earned commendations for teamwork, flexibility and work excellence in providing IT support to students and faculty.

Technology Summary

Certifications	:	Sun Certified Java Developer, Oracle Certified Developer
Systems	:	UNIX, Windows 9X/NT/2000/XP/2K3
Databases	:	Oracle, MySQL, Relational Databases
Languages	:	Visual Basic, SQL, HTML, ASP, CSS, C++, CGI, Perl, Java
Software	:	MS Project, MS Visio, MS Office, Lotus Notes

IT Experience

WIPRO – Bangalore, India

- **Intern,** (2007 to 2008) Handled technical troubleshooting within an enterprise environment, including system crashes, slow-downs and data recoveries. Engaged and tracked Priority 1 issues, with responsibility for the timely documentation, escalation (if appropriate), resolution and closure of trouble tickets.

Selected Contributions:

- Researched and developed knowledge-base articles for travel & expense management issues, resulting in an increase in first-call-resolutions of 20 additional calls per week that saved company Rs 50,000 annually.
- Exceeded issue-resolution targets and achieved exemplary customer satisfaction scores, consistently scoring between 95%-100% on all calls (outperforming average of 90%).
- Handled 30+ technical/mission-critical calls daily and consistently met high service standards.

References available on request

Sample Résumé 2

Srinivas Kamadi

104 Jayabeeri Apartments • Kothaguda, Hyderabad • +91-1234567890 • srinivas.kamadi@example.com

- **Ability to demonstrate the relationship of data structures to systems**
- **Experience analyzing data using SQL**
- **Experience establishing and modifying data models**
- **Strong analytical, organizational, and presentation skills**
- **Experience with Agile, XP, and Lean software development techniques**

- **Experience in a rapidly changing environment due to growth from mergers or acquisitions**

Education

JNT University, Hyderabad - 1995

Technology Summary

Certifications	:	Sun Certified Java Developer, Oracle Certified Developer
Systems	:	UNIX, Windows 9X/NT/2000/XP/2K3
Databases	:	Oracle, MySQL, Relational Databases
Languages	:	Visual Basic, SQL, HTML, ASP, CSS, C++, CGI, Perl, Java
Software	:	MS Project, MS Visio, MS Office, Lotus Notes

IT Experience

2002 - present

Cyberabad Computer Access, Senior Systems Designer

- Develop I/O interfaces and create/support file transfer systems. Extensive use of Java, C++.

1998 – 2002

Crazy Software, Technical Advisor

- Provided marketing and sales support for extensive software product lines including ERP, SCM, and database applications.

1996 - 1998

Finpro Development, Senior Programmer

- Team leader for software development group. Promoted from programmer to senior programmer after one year.

References available on request

Follow up

People forget after applying for the post. You have applied 6 months back and do not get a call letter. If you don't bother about contacting them you are losing the opportunity to others. People consider follow-up might result in negative reaction from the company. This is a myth. You should always keep reminding them. Some of the companies may not respond in your pursuit but never lose heart. Few companies acknowledge the receipt of the application and issue a serial number. It will then become a reference for future correspondence. Note down the application no. and mention about it during telephonic conversation/ email. Personal visit to the company's office, if you are nearby and enquires with HRD may give an idea about the interviews/ selection.

People believe such enquiries will result in keeping their application at abeyance and it will be treated as influencing the authorities. No. Not yet all. One shall be aware of the need of the company and at what stage the processing of application is pending. One can enquire through email or phone. It may fetch good results. You may contact the officer in-charge of recruitment/ HRD.

Keep Good Relationship

The aspirant shall get in touch with the employees working already in the organization and liaison with them. This is called as social network development. Keep on telephoning them and extend your requests. Cultivate them. If you are successful you may get the job. Through your references you may attempt to enrich your résumé. It shall not be in the form of undue recommendation. Majority of the jobs are influenced through political personalities and Board of directors of the company/ institute. Be optimistic till you achieve the goal. Try all means except bribing, which is illegal. Don't try to contact middle men and get deceived. Try through counseling agents and career centers. Keep track of the progress of the company by verifying the prospects of the company through quarterly indexes. The references given are to be genuine. In case the company refers back about your candidature, they shall be able to tell about your back ground, your aptitude. Avoid referring names of politicians, as they may not be able to spend more time when the phone call comes from the company. Simply mentioning the name of a State Minister belonging to your area does not help. It may boomerang.

Career Portals

Enroll your name in career portals. It is one way of getting into the arena of career selection. People do not utilize the technical facility available. By entering your name in a career portal accessibility with the representatives of the company will increase. It will enhance the chances of employment opportunities. Most of the candidates utilize the facilities of internet to forward their résumés. But we cannot forget that it is only one way of communication and it is not the only way to communicate. It is not the end of all. Through leg work one can ascertain the total needs of the company. Get full details and send your bio-data directly to the company. Verify the information available with you, and with your friends also. It is not a secret and the information can be shared though it is competitive in nature. By sharing the information with your friends you may not be losing anything.

Internet

With the help of internet the world has entered into new technological inventions. One can know the latest research findings across the globe in few minutes. Many institutions besides advertisements in news papers, inform through websites, the vacancies. Candidates in search of jobs have to depend mainly on technological information. There are number of methods to send résumé to institutions. Depending on the necessity, candidate can choose any one of them. It is better to know the details of such methods.

Online Job Sites

Plenty of websites options are available before us when we browse the internet for job vacancies. Institutions advertise the vacancy position in websites. Some of the recruitment agencies also invite candidates online for different vacancies in various institutions. They forward applications. They will act as a bridge between candidates and institutions. But we have to opt for reputed recruiting agencies. We have to find out how many are visiting the website. How long they are in the field and the vacancies they are offering to be verified. Find out the rules and regulations. Read the privacy policy of the institution and keep a copy of it.

Social Networks

During the recent times, social network websites have started advertising. Details of job, institution, vacancies in different wings are available on the website. Examine it and forward the résumé. Don't send résumé without collecting information about the institution. If you keep your résumé in it everybody can access it. Do not give personal information in such social networks.

Preparation

There are different types of interviewers. We call them Beginners and Professionals. Beginners are also known as non-professionals. They judge at hand shake. Professional interviewing is about evaluating a candidate in their key areas of strength. Non-professionals have a preset mindset and typically go by things like handshake. A strong handshake for them means confidence and a fish bone is lacking confidence – **Suresh Anubolu, HR Director, Computer Associates**

Interviews are no normal conversations. They are stressful. Believe it or not, they are stressful for the interviewers also. Add to it the fact that perception about the candidate is made at **handshake** and decision made during the first **5-10 minutes**. Another interesting fact is that 70% of the interviewers conducting interviews are not professionally trained to do so. Now mix the combination of analytical, puzzle based and situation questions that the interviewer might put you through in an attempt to evaluate you. More than 50% of the interviewers start the interview by apologizing for not having gone through the résumé and try to do it while talking to you.

Interesting Facts·

Women CEOs in the US Fortune 500 list is pitiably less than 3% ·**Black CEOs** in the Fortune 500 list is less than 1%·**Ursula Burns** becomes the **first black women CEO** of a fortune 500 company and that makes black + women percentage 0.2%

Do the above statistics mean anything? Is it purely coincidence? Does Color or gender make any difference? Now look at this data for sample. 90% of the CEOs in a survey conducted recently were **5 feet 8 inches** and above. Does height and physical appearance also have a bearing on the interview outcome? Do you still call it coincidence? We will figure that out during the course of this book. We will break the myths and put before you facts.

I have been doing campus interviews for 10 years now. I have done it for almost leading business schools. The pressure and stress levels in the business school interviews are high for both candidate and interviewer. For the candidate, there is peer pressure, pressure to perform within a short time and since they would almost be looking for their first job, unlike candidates who are experienced or with engineering background and have a job on hand, they are under pressure to get selected. For the interviewer, he/she has to filter out candidates and make decisions quickly and has to go through large numbers in a day. These are also referred to as **Rejection interviews**. Selection has to be based on his potential and not skills. So he is under stress to select the candidate in a short time. Myself and Chandrasekhar Kakal (Executive member and Unit Head, Infosys) were conducting interviews at a business school and towards end of the day one candidate walked-in and was looking very stressed. So, we asked him if he was stressed. He said "**NO**". He then looking at us said, "**you might also be stressed**" going through so many interviews during the day. Myself and Kakal said, "**we are fine**". Candidate then said, "**Can I sing a song for you?**" It turned out to be a bit embarrassing for both of us. Even before we realized, He stood up, walked to a corner and started singing leaving both of us worried. We were worried as media was waiting outside and we didn't want media to think Infosys is making candidates sing in their interview processHe unfortunately didn't get selected – **Ravi Kumar S, Vice President and Hyderabad Development Center Head, Infosys**

Pre-formed Perceptions

It appears, interviewers form perceptions about job applicants before actually meeting them, from applicant's résumé and human resource forms and other inputs. The dossiers are given to interview panel/board in advance. They frame an impression about the candidate, his education and the background from which he/she comes.

To some extent a smart looking candidate does get an advantage, even if it is sub-conscious – **A.P.V.N Sarma I.A.S, Secretary, Ministry of Shipping (2008-09)**

Physical appearance is very important. He need not be very formal – with suits and ties but should be wearing a formal / semi-formal dress. A very casual dress – multi-colored dress, no shoes etc puts me off. It also demonstrates his preparedness for the meeting, the seriousness attached to the meeting, his intentions of presenting himself – **R K Ravindranath, Vice President, 3i Infotech Software Systems** (Software company)

Physical Appearance of the candidate carries a lot of weight, almost 40%. The percentage goes up to 50% in the case of senior hires. Dressing style, way of greeting, Smile are all important – **Uday Chander, Vice President – People Function, Sierra Atlantic** (Software MNC company)

Perceptions are also formed about candidate based on your experience, kind of company worked for and role played. For instance, if you have worked with a large MNC company like Infosys before, it is but natural for the interviewer to assume you have the necessary skills to carry out the job. That puts you at advantage. What if you have not worked for large companies in the past and now considering making that move? You should look for projects that you have worked on that were large scale, niche technologies or considered complex in nature and highlight those aspects in your résumé.

> I print the résumé 10 minutes before the interview. Look at the company and role he/she has played and if the candidate is from a large company then I give him additional benefit. Otherwise I'm more strict with candidates and trying to evaluate if he would be a fitment – **Ravi Kumar S, Vice President and Hyderabad Development Center Head, Infosys**

Mr. Perfect

Good news is that almost all interviewers believe there is no **Mr. Perfect** for the job they are conducting interviews. They know and believe one can never find an exact match. They consider you **selected,** if you are anywhere **6 to 8 on a scale of 10.** Does that help boost your morale? It is important to thing about those positive aspects about the interview when facing one. Companies understand that. So, never considering not applying for a job thinking you don't have all the qualities they have listed in the job description posted in the AD or on their website. Don't believe?

> 6-8 is my average hiring score – **Feroze Mohammed, SVP Global Delivery, Sierra Atlantic** (Software Company)
>
> 10 on 10 are very RARE. – **Suresh Anubolu, HR Director, Computer Associates**
>
> Have never come across a 10 ON 10. A job applicant we hired was only 7 on 10 but had qualities that we were looking for. Candidate had extreme passion for what he was doing at school and he had good academics and all round overall exposure and is currently working with us. He is almost one of us – **Ravi Vankamamidi, Chief Solutions Officer, S3Edge** (Software Company)

Right Job

"Getting a job is easy. Getting the right job is not"

Finding a job is easy but is that your dream job is the question you should be asking. You can pick-up an axe and walk into a forest and become a woodchopper any day or you can open a small pan shop next door and make money. Is that your dream job? Would you be motivated to do that? Hence, landing in the right job at the right time is the key to success. Find a job where you don't wake up in the morning and think "why am I going to office today?" So, it is all about

AandA

Ability and Aspiration.

What are your abilities? For instance, if you are in software development field, are you up to date in your programming skills? Are you a Java/J2EE resource with knowledge of what is latest in that space? Did you undergo trainings in Web Services, SOA, Rich Internet Applications? Are you certified in Java/J2EE architecture?

What are your aspirations? Are you currently with a small company and want to move to a Multi National Company? Are you currently an Oracle developer and would like to work for Oracle directly? May be you are in a small town and would want to move to a big city like Bangalore or Hyderabad? Is your aspiration to go to the USA and work there?

Definition of right job would depend on your ability and aspirations.

> Great golfers don't hit the ball with eyes closed but take time to consider exactly where they are going to hit the ball, taking into account how the contours of the course will affect the way ball will bounce and roll. In essence, it is called "**walk the golf course**". In our parlance, it should be "**talk to yourself**" to understand your abilities and aspirations

Self Analysis

Before you attend an interview, you should perform self analysis of yourself. As a candidate applying for job, Interview is a process of selling yourself to the company. You as the sales man should know your strengths and weaknesses very well.

How to know your strengths?

An easy way to assess your strengths is to think of those tasks that you excelled doing, those you enjoyed doing, those that were appreciated by others, those that gave you pride of achievement and inner satisfaction. It could be about organizing, fast decision making, planning, team building, innovation or ability to take pressure at work.

Few examples

- Got 100 out of 100 in applied mathematics paper in my Engineering
- My paper on "Project management in uncertain times" got selected for a conference in the USA
- First prize in Table tennis championship at college level

> **Do it yourself**
> Spend 10 minutes thinking of your strengths and write them down

Common Sense

Interviews are stressful situations and research shows that when you are under stress you tend to lose your common sense and answer even questions that are simple and easy to answer incorrectly. You don't believe us. Take the below test and we ask you to perform the below steps before taking our interview questions. Assume you are facing an interview and you have to answer next questions "only" after you have answered the previous.

Q1: What do you put in a toaster?

If your answer was **BREAD** then you obviously got it wrong. If your answer was bread, pls move on. This question was intentionally made easy. Like all interviews this also started with an easy one. We want you to relive your interview experience.

Q2: Say "Silk" five times. Now spell "Silk". What do cows drink?

If you have said **MILK** then take a break before you take the next question.

Q3: There is a very tall coconut tree and 4 animals (Lion, Monkey, Giraffe and Squirrel). They decide to compete and find out who is the first to get a banana off the tree.

If you said Giraffe or **MONKEY** or Squirrel the answer is WRONG. LION is obviously also WRONG. Coconut tree doesn't have bananas.

Q4: If a red house is made of red bricks, blue house made of blue bricks, pink house made of pink bricks and black house made from black bricks. What is green house made from?

If you said **GREEN**, go watch a movie, read some jokes and come back. Green houses are made from glass.

ALMOST everyone fails these tests. If you have answered all these basic questions correctly then you are among the 5% individuals who apply common sense even in stressful situations.

Soft Skills Assessment

Interviewers are known to use different tools and techniques to evaluate candidates around soft skills and behavior. As they say attitude of the candidate drives his behavior on the job. Unfortunately, that is the most difficult thing to judge for an interviewer. Interviewer hence might use STAR or BEI (Behavioral Event based Interview) technique. We have provided ample questions and answers in the 101 section that deal with this technique.

Interview process is like an iceberg. In other words, we only see 10-20% of the iceberg above the sea level and the rest 80-90% is below the sea (invisible to naked eye). It is the other 80-90% (candidate's attitude, ethics, motives and beliefs) that drives the other 10-20%. Applying the same analogy to interview selection process, interviewer will use the 10-20% and predict candidate's future behavior based on that 10-20% assessment made in the interview.

There is another interesting data point to prove the same. If we were to represent each letter below with the numerical equivalent of the same (based on its position in the alphabetical sequence), attitude gets a 100 score in comparison to the others like SKILLS, KNOWLEDGE and HARD WORK.

S	K	I	L	L	S	
19	11	9	12	12	19	=82

K	N	O	W	L	E	D	G	E	
11	14	15	23	12	5	4	7	5	=96

H	A	R	D	W	O	R	K	
8	1	12	4	23	15	18	11	=98

A	T	T	I	T	U	D	E	
1	20	20	9	20	21	4	5	=100

In other words, to be successful in life or interview you need to have the right attitude. More and more interviewers today look for attitude of the candidate. As they say, "**Attitude** not your **aptitude** decides your **altitude**"

> I hire for Soft skills and not necessarily content/technology
>
> (1) Maneuverability – Ability to network through the organization and get things done. This is very important in large organizations where you would never be responsible for end to end and hence have to influence others to move along with you
>
> (2) Communication – His ability to articulate
>
> (3) Coherent and Logical reasoning – Should be able to reason out well and in line with the detail being provided by the candidate– **Ravi Kumar S, Vice President and Hyderabad Development Center Head, Infosys**
>
> (1) The first is intellectual integrity. Any bluffing or knowingly telling any wrong or incorrect information makes a candidate completely unsuitable. Probing questions do elicit "*I don't know*" response and there the interviewer can judge the integrity of the candidate.
>
> (2) The quality of a lively interest in what's happening around and how these events affect our lives is a very important one and is needed for a civil servant. An empathy with the common man is also part of this. Questions on current developments in the political, economic and social sectors enable us to assess this quality in a candidate.
>
> (3) Deep appreciation of developments in one's own field of academic studies and again how they relate to our lives is another important quality. The interviewer has to do some homework in advance to lead a meaningful discussion in this area.
>
> **– A.P.V.N Sarma I.A.S, Secretary, Ministry of Shipping (2008-09)**

Interview Rounds

Like a full course meal (3 course or 12 course), interview also has different rounds. While a full course meal differs based on how formal the setting is, interview rounds depend on the type of job, company size, experience and industry. Some companies have just 2 rounds – 1 technical and 1 HR round. While others can have as many as 7-8 rounds – Screening round, Analytical round, multiple technical rounds, management round and HR selection round. Most companies today rely on at least one of the interview rounds being face to face. In case face to face cannot be organized (because the candidate is in a different country), companies are using video conferencing technologies to conduct the same.

Big successful companies have multiple rounds of interviews. Companies like Microsoft, Oracle and Google are known to have 6-8 rounds of interviews based on what level and role you are applying for. These can be tiring and time consuming. We advise you to be patient and ask the interviewer in the first round to explain the process, number of round they would be conducting and the time it would take for them to make a decision. This removes any anxiety you might otherwise be carrying. There is no harm in asking the interviewer to explain the process.

Interview Stages

There are 3 main stages in the interview.

(1) Starters - Comfort Stage

This is the ice-breaker phase. Interviewer tries to make the candidate feel at home by trying to talk about common interest topics.

This is the ice-breaker phase. Interviewer tries to make the candidate feel at home by trying to talk about common interest topics.

> I ask candidate about his company, offer him/her coffee and tea. For instance, I say, Let us walk & pick up a coffee/tea
>
> **– Suresh Anubolu, HR Director, Computer Associates**
>
> I ask him for brief introduction, offering him / her seat, glass of water, coffee. A minute of little chit chat to break the ice etc. Instead of jumping into the subject, casually ask about the candidate, what does he / she do etc. which eases their nerves
>
> **- R K Ravindranath, Vice President, 3i Infotech Software Systems** (Software company)

(1) Main Course - Competency Probing Stage

This stage is where interviewer tries to use CASE, BEI or STAR techniques to assess the candidate.

(2) Desserts - Closing Stage

This stage is where interviewer has finished his assessment and opens it up for any questions from the candidate. You might hear interviewer saying "Do you have any questions for me?"

On asked if "We will get back to you" in the closing stage means rejection in interviews

NO. I communicate Yes or NO directly than use "we will get back to you". Also, talk about the next steps involved in the hiring process

- Feroze Mohammed, SVP Global Delivery, Sierra Atlantic
(Software Company)

Not a negative statement. If the next steps are not clear then it means you are rejected. If the discussion is about compensation, when you can join or you will meet one more interviewer then you have high chances of getting selected otherwise you are in the doubtful list

– Ravi Kumar S, Vice President and Hyderabad Development Center Head, Infosys

No. This is more to do with immaturity of the interviewer

– Suresh Anubolu, HR Director, Computer Associates

NO – It is always a group that decides on the interview. Hence, we cannot any case decide on the selection on our own and say we will get back to you

– Ravi Vankamamidi, Chief Solutions Officer, S3Edge
(Software Company)

Group Discussion (GD)

Group discussion technique is used in interviews to filter out people. To save time, when there are large number of candidates, companies use GD technique to reject candidates and shortlist the good ones from them. Topic selection is based on the type of interview and job you are attending. Candidates are given 5-10 minutes to prepare and pool their thoughts.

3 Important qualities to be successful in a GD

- Clarity in thought and expression
- Good listening and

Assertiveness and Appreciation

(1) Clarity

You should be able to express your thoughts fluently and fearlessly. There is a mad rush in the beginning to express your thought. Everyone is trying to impress initially to make their point. Wait for your turn and speak slowly, confidently and with clarity. Always, think before you speak. Reading a lot of newspapers, magazines, journals and business articles helps you present your view point. You can also quote popular authors/articles when making your point. That goes to show your subject knowledge. Sometimes controversial topics are chosen for discussion. It is always better to be prepared to take questions and comments from other participants in the discussion when you are presenting a radical thought or view that is completely different from others.

(2) Good Listener

Being attentive helps you either support or reject the point made by other participants of GD. It also helps you choose different view point than what is already being discussed. If you are not listening carefully to the discussion and worrying about what you are going to say, it is quite possible that you end up speaking about the same point that has already been beaten to death in the discussion.

(3) Assertive and Appreciative

You need to be both assertive and appreciative in the discussion. Keep in mind not to be seen as over aggressive.

How not to be over assertive?

- You can do that by agreeing to some extent with the other participant but also presenting your view point. You can start by saying… "I agree to some extent but I also believe…"
- Addressing the group and not taking on one participant in the group. Avoid making it personal and brining emotions into the topic

How to be appreciative?

- Take the name of the individual who has presented a good view point and appreciate him/her
- Allowing others to make their view point as well

> **Do it yourself**
>
> Choose a current topic and try presenting point of view both supporting and against the topic of discussion. Do some research first, then use that as reference in your articulation

Interviewer Types

Each interviewer carries with him different experience, background, motives & needs. Unfortunately you don't have the choice of deciding the interviewer. Interviewer can have very little experience and no formal training or an expert with formal training on how to conduct the interview. In the following sections we teach you how to deal with each one of them successfully.

(1) HR Generalist

These don't carry the subject matter expertise but are good at short-listing and filtering out candidates. Some of them do carry breadth in industry knowledge or specific skill area but lack depth. They are generally professionals in conducting interviews with formal training. You need something catchy to get their attention. You need to showcase your **VALUE** to the organization and role. To sell VALUE, you need to understand the need. Find out more detail about the opening in the organization, type of experience and profile they are in the lookout for. It is always a good idea to keep information handy by categorizing your experience based on your industry, role, experience, and company size. Listen carefully to the description provided by the HR generalist and then carefully explain your relevant experience and the VALUE you can bring to their organization.

Use this interview to find out more information, like

- What is the interview procedure in their company?
- Who will be speaking next and what is his/her title and name?
- More about their company and the role

(2) Hiring Manager

This person is typically going to be your boss (if you were to get selected). Unlike the HR Generalist, he is more technical in your area of expertise and would be making the hiring decision. This type of interviewer lacks formal training and don't have in-depth knowledge of the company and different divisions. They only know their division or department very well. Hiring manager would like to know how well you can fill the gap in his organization, how quickly you can adopt yourself into his group, your relevant experience in their area of work and can he/she rely on you to be his team member.

(3) Lunch/Dinner interviews

Senior management position interviews typically happen over a meal. They are informal settings and hence you are required to take care of few things before you head out. While the setting might be informal; don't doubt the seriousness of the interviewer or the interview process.

- Order food that you are comfortable eating
- Avoid liquor/alcohol (especially if it is a lunch meeting)
- Select a seat that is away from the crowd or less noisy
- Thank the interviewer for his choice of restaurant, food or place
- Be clear and confident on your table etiquette

(4) Tele/Video interviews

In the situations where a face to face interview cannot be organized, companies now prefer conducting interviews over telephone or video/ web camera. Each one of them has its own set of benefits and challenges.

Telephonic interviews

- Use landline number to receive calls. If you only have a mobile number, then take the interview from a place where the signal is good and voice clear.
- Avoid long pauses in the interview. Interviewer might confuse it with you seeking answers to the interview question over internet or in a book
- Don't proxy for others.

Web Cam interviews

- Ensure you have good internet broadband connection. Test the connectivity before the interview
- Keep a separate telephone line as standby. Preferably use a separate line for voice and video
- Look straight into the camera and talk as if you are having a eye to eye contact
- Sit in a comfortable posture and set the camera to focus on your face

Interview Gyan (Wisdom) – 10 "*Commandments*" to Success

<u>Gyan 1</u> : **Interview Questions 101 (section below) are not meant for memorizing**

<u>Gyan 2</u> : **You can succeed in interview by preparing well**

<u>Gyan 3</u> : **Check your resume to ensure there are no mistakes (even simple spelling mistakes)**

<u>Gyan 4</u> : **Your attitude not aptitude defines your altitude**

<u>Gyan 5</u> : **Your dressing and appearance matters to the interviewers**

<u>Gyan 6</u> : **"We will get back to you" doesn't mean rejection**

<u>Gyan 7</u> : **Be coherent and clear in your responses**

<u>Gyan 8</u> : **SELL yourself. Don't feel bad to praise yourself. Interview is all about YOU**

<u>Gyan 9</u> : **Be pleasant and have a smile on your face**

<u>Gyan 10</u> : **There is never a 10 on 10. You don't need to be 100% qualified to apply for the job.**

5

Interview Process

"Life is a stair case and not an escalator. You have to walk up; you won't get pushed up."

- H.L. Davis

Purpose of Interview

The interview board mainly assesses the personality of a candidate for psychological traits and sociological qualities. It is a form of communication in which the candidate interacts through question-answer session for specific goals. Display of knowledge acquired through study of newspapers and magazines in the interview is not enough.

Interviewer has a chance to look into the other's hidden qualities. Candidate puts forth his past and present incidents, feelings and reactions to the interview board. Interview is a formal meeting aimed at finding one's suitability for the job. It is a social process between interviewer and interviewee. It brings out the inner qualities and traits of the candidate.

The interview board may consist of one or more number of persons. They try to know the outlook and characteristics of the candidate in a limited time frame. In this social process a rapport is established between the two. **If the candidate is not willing to come out of his shell no body can help.** The board makes the candidate feel comfortable at the interview.

IMPRESSION MANAGEMENT

Our efforts to make a good impression on others are known as impression management or self presentation. The desire to make a favorable impression on others is a strong one, so most of us do our best to look good to others when we meet them for the first time. These efforts are worth the trouble. Persons who can perform impression management successfully do often gain important advantages in many situations.

Self Enhancement

In includes efforts to improve our own appearance. This can be accomplished through alterations in dress, through personal grooming, through the judicious use of non verbal cues.

Other Enhancement

Efforts to make the target person feel good in our presence are important. The most important of these tactics are flattery-heaping praise on target persons, expressing agreement with their views, showing a high degree of interest in them and expressing liking for them either verbally or non verbally.

Social psychologists say that the decision as to weather to put these tactics to use is an ethical one that individual must reach for themselves.

A person well dressed is widely respected in society, a person with good conversation gets on well and the last one is God given Physical personality. We can cultivate good conversation and dress properly. The physical characteristics cannot be improved. However the impression one gests at the first appearance is the most crucial one.

Your Appearance

Candidates preparing for job interview either for civil services or others, dress or groom themselves as carefully as possible. Every one knows that appearance really matters where first impressions are concerned. Researchers suggest that such beliefs as well founded. Interviewers' ratings of job applicants are influenced by the applicant's appearance and factors relating to this. Attractive persons have an edge over less attractive ones. Similarly persons who dress for interviews in a manner considered appropriate by interviewers often receive higher ratings than persons who dress in a less appropriate manner.

Interviewers often assign higher ratings to applicants who emit high levels of non verbal cues – persons who smile, nod and lean forward frequently during an interview. The outcome of interviews is often influenced by aspects of applicant's appearance over which they exert direct control. Perhaps even more unsettling is evidence indicating that such effects also occur for variables over which individuals have relatively little control-factors such as gender and being overweight.

Expectancy Confirmation in Job Interviews

We perceive and actually get what we expect to get. It appears, interviewers form expectancies about job applicants before actually meeting them, from applicant's personnel and human resource forms and other inputs. The dossiers are given to the assessors of the interview board in advance. They frame an impression about the candidate, his education and the background from which he/she comes.

Sometimes a simple question answered badly gives a wrong signal. At an All India competition I asked a candidate about the language spoken in Tamil Nadu. He replied positively. When I asked about the language spoken in Kerla he said it is Keralam on the similar lines of Tamil. The commonsense is appreciated but the inadvocacy of his basic knowledge was evident. The common question asked is how he or she is best suited for the job in question. The applicant should be prepared for this type of question in befitting manner. In contrast they may ask more searching and fewer supportive questions, may emit negative non verbal cues, and may focus on examining applicant qualifications and past experience. In most cases the applicant furnish out of enthusiasm more experience and when they are interrogated they fail to answer properly and prove themselves at the wrong side. Similarly about there degrees which they acquire from distance education centers, which supply degrees liberally. On one occasion it was found a candidate possessing post graduate diploma at the age of 16. A bogus certificate, indeed.

Experiences play an important role in job interviews, just as they do in many other social situations. Applicants who look good on paper before the interview may find themselves facing an interviewer who is largely on their side and who engages in actions that help them do their best. In contrast, applicants whose records are unimpressive may find themselves facing an interviewer who acts as adversary-one who seems to say, in many different ways, **"ok. Show me why I should recommend you for this Job?". The candidate should be well prepared for this.**

Why are Interviews so Scary?

Have you ever felt jittery before an interview? Nervous or even terrified? Have you ever wished you had answered a question differently or negotiated your salary more skillfully? Do you panic when you imagine the possibility of "failure"? Do you just want to make sure you get it right the first time?

Interviews are not like normal conversations. Being interviewed can be scary, even for ordinary outgoing people. When you are sitting in the hot seat, the interviewer is an authority figure, and he or she has all or most of the power in the interview.

An Assault Against Anxiety

The most common fears the people have voiced about interviewing are listed below. Many of us learned in childhood or later that "Blowing your own horn" is a sign of being on an ego trip. But providing information about the nature of work you have done is not doing that. It is simply stating the facts.

(1) Everyone says I am under / overqualified. What should I do?

Usually the employer who says he or she is worried about either of these issues actually has a hidden agenda. We talk about **"Questions behind questions".**

(2) What should I do if an interviewer asks me an intrusive or illegal question?

Some topics, such as disabilities, martial status are off-limits during an interview.

(3) I don't know what to do with my hands during an interview:

This is a very common worry. Once you know the one most potent secret of nonverbal behavior in an interview, you'll find your hands will just fall into place, and you won't even have to think about them.

(4) I fear I will just "Freeze up" in the interview:

You'll learn the technique of "stalling and accessing", which is a convincing and comfortable way out of this one. It will seem very natural, once you learn it.

(5) I had to answer technical questions:

They were easy, and I knew I had answered them right. The interviewer said I answered them wrong. What do I do in a situation like that? Sound familiar? If you're an engineer or scientist, you've very likely faced this type of scenario. It can be unnerving.

(6) Do I have to reveal how much money I made at my last job?

(7) How and when should I bring up the issue of salary?

Not only you shall be able to handle salary discussions, you shall be able to master them.

The Morning of the Interview

A good night's sleep should be priority before this important morning because there is much to do before 10.00 A.M. interview. The morning hours should be focused on preparing to make an excellent first impression. There is only one chance for this to happen. Visualize positive interaction between you and interviewers and you will convey good feelings and improve the odds of a positive outcome. If you speak with anyone on the morning of the interview, make sure that the person is supportive, positive and upbeat.

> **Pretend you are about to attend a martial arts lesson on how to defend yourself against someone with a baseball bat. Get that adrenalin flowing. Bet alert, feel good about yourself. Be relaxed and maintain your inner confidence. You can do it.**

Get Dressed for Success

Conservative clothing is in and beach things are out. First impressions are formed mostly by nonverbal communications including appearance, facial expression, eye contact, posture, and least of all, spoken words. Before you utter a single word, your appearance already has. First impressions are formed within thirty seconds, many times subliminally.

> **According to Joanne Pobiner, Certified Image Consultant and professional member of the Association of image consultants international (AICI), "significant value judgments are made based solely upon appearance, for example, economic status, education, level of success, sophistication, integrity, credibility, likeability, and even moral character. The visual integrity of job seekers is clearly at stake.**

Casual business dress often turns out to be casuality dress in interview situations. Remember that you are not yet an employee, and you must go through a hazing period before you are permitted to dress like one. Styles vary by profession as well as region of the country. If you are interviewed for a job in the advertising or entertainment industries, you may be able to dress less formally than in the financial services industry or legal profession.

Check the Department's web site or annual report of the Department/Ministry that is interviewing you. View pictures of the management team. The most important aspect about you appearance for an interview is that you think you look great. If you look and feel great, your heightened self-confidence will likely make a favorable impression upon your interviewer.

- **The best advice for smokers interviewing for an office position is to stop smoking on the day of interview when looking for a job. It is almost impossible to hide the smell.**
- **Avoid perfume or use it very sparingly. Why chance an embarrassing sneezing fit?**

Get there Early

Plan to arrive at the place of interview 30 minutes before the scheduled interview, otherwise you will be stressed and lose advantage for a positive first impression. Go to the location so that you will know exactly where it is, and walk or drive to the nearest coffee shop or eating establishment and just relax for half an hour. Review your notes from the research; think positive thoughts about the upcoming interview. Before you leave the coffee shop, go to the rest room and take a last minute look at yourself, particularly you smile. That will be your most widely used weapon during the interview, so make sure there are no food remains. Arrive at the reception desk about ten minutes before the scheduled time.

In an interview it is your opportunity to tell an employer what you've accomplished in the past and how you'll help them in the future.

Last-Minute Preparation

Before you leave home for the interview, make sure you have everything you need. Interviewer and receptionist names, address, telephone number, and directions to the place are critical. Take a note pad and carry ballpoint pen. Bring three copies of your resume, but offer it only if asked. The notepad and selected reference material about the department should be placed in a folder.

Buy the morning news paper and read the headlines and the current affairs section for interesting, non-controversial stories that might be brought up in the course of conversation.

Get Ready for Fearless Interviewing

Knowing your strengths, provide concrete examples of those strengths, building the lasting confidence to present yourself and your skills in the best possible light.

· What interviewers are really looking for?
· How to charm your way into the interviewer's heart in the first 20 seconds of the interview
· How to express your strengths and skills with power and laser like precision.

- How to handle even the most difficult questions.
- How to use body language in your favor.
- The most important questions to ask the employer.
- How to be a master at negotiating your salary.

Body Language

Listen carefully to the questions. Your replies should focus on your position to meet the needs of the job.

Good listening is more important, than simply interrupting the interviewers. Pay full attention. Establish good eye contact and nod after every statement from the interviewer.

> **Unknowingly you will be conveying your doubts and fears along with your thoughts. Your body language may be negative, even contradictory to your thoughts. Get well prepared with answers and do not fail to convince your interviewers.**

- Disagree pleasantly. Maintain a friendly tone while replaying and keep a relaxed posture.
- Defensive body language such as folded arms or crossed legs is to be avoided.
- When you are making an important point, do not stare. Look at the interviewer in the eye.
- Be comfortable and relaxed. Don't give the impression of being tense or desperate for the job. Be alert and attentive.
- Interviewers may sometime put the candidate under stress to gauge their ability to handle the situation. It is important what you say and how you say. It will show how well you can handle a crisis.

> **The door of opportunity won't open unless you do some pushing. Push yourself.**

Let us go in detail item by item:

Personal Interview

Rule of the Game

Personal interview is basically an attempt to asses the mental ability of the candidate. Different recruiting agencies follow different rules of the Game. Filtration at different stages after screening tests is done meticulously. At the time of personal interviews the procedure followed is discussed here.

UPSC (Union Public Service Commission)

The largest recruiting agency in the country has an year long calendar for examinations and personal interviews. They publish the calendar well in advance and follow a regular procedure for conducting the exams as per schedule. Different centers for conducting the examinations through out the country are notified for the convenience of the candidates.

The results of the examinations are announced as per schedule and personal interviews conducted. II class rail fares are reimbursed for the candidates called for interview.

The personal interview board includes one member of UPSC as Chairman and three advisors from different specializations to assist and advise the committee. Normally the interview will be for a duration of 25 to 30 mts for each candidate. Language interpreter helps the candidate and the commission in translating questions and replies.

The shortlist of candidates will be announced through news papers and UPSC website. The selections are made through fool proof method.

Fluency in English

The art of communication is different. One may be fluent in his own mother tongue. He is capable in communicating in his own language. His handicap is to get the thought content translated into English.

To avoid all such complications the UPSC introduced interpreters for the benefit of candidates. Candidates have the choice either to reply fully or partly in English or to opt for mother tongue. The interpreter helps him. But the interpreter has no say in the selection process. He is like an interpreter to two Prime Ministers / Presidents of different countries. He will not be part of the policy making or agreements signed between two counties. After the interview part of a particular candidate is over interpreter is asked to leave the room for few minutes so that the members of the board can discuss and arrive at a conclusion to grade the candidate and allot marks.

Previous Night

While preparing for the personal interview avoid overnight studies during the previous day. Mentally you may not be able to with stand next day. It may lead to confusion.

- Read select topics.
- Rehearse your way of replies the previous night.
- Take the help of senior / elders during Rehearsal.
- Sleep early by 9 to 10pm.
- Remember statistics.
- Avoid taking Tea, Coffee in Exams.
- Avoid taking liquor (If you are in the habit).
- Do not take heavy food.
- Do not by heart answers.
- Jot down some hints in a dairy to verify before interview.
- Go through the dairy of events.

Morning of Interview Day : [The D – Day]

- Get up early.
- Finish your daily chores.
- Take light breakfast.
- Reach place of interview 1 hr in advance.
- Check up all the relevant papers to be shown.
- Dress up properly.
- Avoid going by crowded buses.
- **Relax, Relax and Relax**
- Wait for your turn – in interview.
- Avoid gossiping in the corridors.
- Avoid prolonged discussions with other candidates.
- Do not show off.
- Go to coffee house.
- Watch your face in the mirror.
- Check up the tie (if you are wearing. Tie is not compulsory.)
- Check up shoe laces, if wearing.
- Clean your face if you have eaten in the canteen.
- Dress your hair properly/ modestly.

- Do not go with empty stomach.
- Keep your papers ready.
- Have a small kit to place your papers.
- Keep your publications ready.
- Keep your experience certificates ready.
- Show your degree/ qualification certificates.
- Collect them back.
- Fill up your travel reimbursement sheet.
- Take 3 recent passport size photos with you.
- Take letter from present employee, if employed.
- Information to be updated, it necessary.
- Do not leave the place for smoking/ pissing
  Just 5 to 10 mts before your call.
  (If necessary inform the attendant)
- Keep a smiling face.
- Avoid worries and last minute tension.
- Avoid spicy food two hours in advance.

Dress Code

There is no dress code for any personal interview. You can improve your communication skills like speech, body language. Dressing is completely in your hands. There is no rule book regarding dress.

Stress Code : Avoid stress. Practice meditation. There are two cardinal dates / days in your career building

1. The examination day 2. Personal Interview day.

Some hints are given in general. They are not real situations. It depends upon the level of candidate's mental and physical ability.

- Keep your mind cool.
- Keep silence for at least an hour in advance.
- Don't watch T.V. Serials.
- Take light food.
- Check up your B.P. Levels / Sugar levels (If you are prone)
- Don't strain your self.
- Avoid hurrying up to examination hall.
- Reach the examination center 30 min in advance.

- Go through the notes you have prepared.
- Check your pocket before invigilator checks.
- Go to wash room 15 min in advance.
- Sit Quiet and calm in the examination hall – 10 min ahead.
- Verify your hall ticket number and write down.
- Don't get nervous.
- Don't feel that question paper is difficult.
- Don't feel that questions are out of syllabus.
- Read the second side of the question paper.
- Feel that other candidates are also sailing in the same boat.
- Space out answering schedule as per time available.
- Check up answers at the last.
- Verify once again the hall ticket number.
- Leave last 5 min for overall review.
- **Relax, Relax and Relax.**

Avoid Mannerisms

This is the time when lady luck smiles on you. The 20 to 30 mt. interview is the time for you to show your capacities. Your entire future is decided on how you act your role in a prescribed game plan. It can be unlucky if you miserably fail. **Avoid frequent use of "Sorry Sir, I have no idea, yes sir, No Sir, Excuse me sir, kindly repeat Sir, I am not able to recollect" type of phrases.** Similarly nodding the head I keeping your tongue open to express sorry, leaning on the table, laughing etc., will give a bad impression to the Board.

While entering the Board Room wish the persons sitting across the table. Occupy the Chair allotted for you with grace. Do not sit cross legged. Do not keep your legs one above the other as if you are the boss. Do not sit in a relaxed mood. Similarly do not express anxiety, restlessness at the time of answering. If you feel like taking a glass of water, if available on the table take it. Do not gulp it. Don't take too much time to drink water.

If coffee / tea is offered do not gulp it. Take it with table manners. Pencil / Pen for Jotting down points can be of much help to you. When it is necessary only use them. Avoid dropping names of senior Officials / Politicians during your answers. It is not well taken. If a mention about references that you have made figure in the interview you mention the way how you know him / her.

Talk continuously in English / Telugu / Hindi. Do not mixe up all the three languages. Opt regional language if you are shaky in answering in English / Hindi. **This is a stepping stone for success.** Interview is the main criteria for the Board to know about you. You may be more intelligent and have scored marks well, but personal interview is to Judge your capacities. **Pray God and play well.**

> **Avoid repetition of same statistics, figures, phrases and information. It is not important – what you know but what you communicate and how you communicate to the numbers.**

Body Language

If the interviewer extends his hand to greet, extend your hand. Keep eye to eye contact. Offer greeting with shake hand firmly but do not crush his hand. Your hands may be damp but it does not matter.

When you enter the interview room, wait for a while till you are offered the chair by the Chairman of the Board. If there are two or more chairs vacant left out sit direct to interviewer with great confidence.

Start smiling. Greet them by saying Good Morning /Good afternoon/ Good evening depending on the time.

Typical Interview Questions

Candidates shall be prepared to face some typical questions at the beginning. First impression is the best impression. After salutations / greetings by the candidate and occupying the chair, normally the Chair person starts the ball rolling in the interview. **What is in a name? But in interviews everything is in a 'name'.**

Chairman : Hello Murali! Your name is Murali. What does it mean? Can you explain.

Answer : Murali is the flute of Lord Krishna.

Similar questions based on the names of the candidate are as follows: He shall be able to explain the puranic / cultural meaning.

These are only illustrative and candidate has to answer appropriately.

Father's Name: According to Tamil tradition the surname will be name of his father: R. Srinivasan, Ramaswami Srinivasan etc. If questioned the tradition of adding father's name as surname is to be explained. If the father's name has any peculiarity it is to be explained shortly. If the name of the father is illustratious, associated with any freedom fighter like Rajagopalachari, Bhakta Vatsalam etc. it is to be informed.

Surnames: As per the tradition in Andhra Pradesh and several other states the village name will be surname. The question may be on the population of the place Ex. Nellore. (Famous for a variety of rice called Nellore Rice. Varanasi, (famous Viswanadh Temple) Duggirala (Free dom fighter Duggirala Gopalakrishnaiah) etc.

Place of Birth: In the application candidate fills his birth place. If the place is popular or associated with a famous personality, the answer shall contain relevant information.

Ex. Vijayawada: Place of Kanadurga temple and famous for river Krishna. Freedom fighter and Central Irrigation Minister Dr. K.L. Rao represented the constituency in Loksabha followed by Sri Gode Murahari, Chairman, Rajya Sabha. Harindranath Chattopadyaya, famous writer also represented it in Loksabha.

(2) Kurukshetra : Tourist place in Haryana. Associated with Mahabharath war between evil and Dharma - Kowravas and Pandavas. Lord Sri Krishna counseled Arjuna at Kurukshetra with Bhagavadgita, the Holy scripture.

(3) Ujjain : The famous Sanskrit poet Mahakavi Kalidasa composed many epics like Raghuvamsa and play Shakuntalam. Mahakali of Ujjain is a famous diety.

(4) Kanchi : The seat of learning of Adi Shankara who established four peethas in four parts of the country. He lived only for 32 years and toured all over India.

States of Birth: North East candidates have to be thorough with North East Policy. South Indian Candidates shall be thorough with the historical cultural political importance of the states. North Indian candidates shall be aware of the tourist / political Geographical importance of their native state. Candidates from the newly formed states in 2000 like Uttarakhand, Jharkhand, and Chattisgarh face lot of questions. Historical political reasons for states reorganization is to be illustrated. Supplementary can be whether further states bifurcation is advisable and what is your opinion? Candidates from Andhra, UP, Maharashtra shall be able to infirm about sentiment of Regionalism and agitations for smaller states. Candidates from Union Territories like Andaman, Nicobar, Chandigarh etc shall explain the Administrative set up in Union Territories.

Lengthy Names: Mostly South Indian Candidates have lengthy names and when abbreviated it goes like this:

APVN Sarma (1974 AP), MVPC Sastry (1977 AP), IYR Krishna Rao (1979 AP).

CVSK Sarma (1980 AP) CBSV Ramana (1982 AP), GSRCV Prasada Rao (1982).

JSV Prasad (1987 TN) KAV Setty (1983 TN) VA Shegaonkar (1985 TN).

ARC Gupta (1976 KN) AKC Manoli (1982 KN).

Candidates shall be prepared to explain the reason for lengthy names in a reasonable manner. Mostly each letter denotes a God / family God / Father's / Grand father's name. The tradition of Christening the child with Grand father's name in south is to be explained.

Explanation of certain names :

Manikanta	:	Person wearing Jewell in his neck. Name of Lord Ayyappa.
Veerabhadra	:	Son of Lord Siva who destroyed Dakshayajna.
Gurucharan	:	Person with respectful feet.
Jagadeesh	:	King of earth.
Raghavendra	:	Lord Rama; Diety at Mantralaya famous Madhva Acharya.

This is only illustrative and not exhaustive list.

Agnihotri	:	God Agni (Fuel)
Viswanadh	:	Lord Siva, Diety of Kashi – Kashi Viswanath
Narasimham	:	One of the Dasavataras – Ten manifestations of Lord Vishnu. Narasimha killed Hiranya Kasipa father of Prahlada.
Bhanu Pratap	:	Sun God. Pratap denotes valour. Valour of Sun.
Bhima Sankaram	:	Powerful Siva. Nothing to do with Bhima of Pancha Pandavas.
Durga Prasad	:	Gifted by Goddess Durga.
Bramahaji	:	The creator of human beings (Lord Bramhan)
Chandra Sekhar	:	Lord Siva wearing Moon on his head.
Gopala Krishna	:	Lord Krishna associated with Gopalas of Nanda Gokulam.
Nagaraju	:	The serpent king – Adisesha.
Padmakar	:	Pond of Lotus flowers.
Tataji	:	South Indian name for grand father. (Also Industrialist Tata)
Mohan	:	Beautiful person.
Jagannadham	:	Diety of Puri (Orissa State)
Umanath	:	Lord Siva, husband of Uma (Parvati)
Venugopal	:	Lord Krishna with his flute – venu.
Syamsundar	:	Lod Krishna, beautiful with dark skin.
Ravi Kiran	:	Rays of Sun.
Vikramaditya	:	King of Chola ynasty
Tilak	:	Freedom fighter Bal Gangadhar Tilak
Hemasundar	:	Beautiful as Gold.

Chakravarti : King of Kings
Aravind : Aurabindo of Pondicherry, spiritual lader. (Name of a flower)
Seshagiri : Mountain named affer Adisesha. (One of the seven hills of Tirumala).
Rajeswar : Name of Lord Siva — Raja + Eswar.
Sameer Kumar : Son of Lord Vayu (Hanuman)
Anil Kumar : Son of Lord Vayu (Hanuman)
Pavan Kumar : Son of Lord Vayu (Hanuman)

Lady Names :

Anuradha	:	One of the 27 clestical stars – Ashwini – etc.
Annapurna	:	Godess of Kashi – Known for serving food to all.
Aruna	:	Reddish colour.
Aparna	:	Godess Parvati who stopped taking even leaves also as food during her penance.
Chaya	:	Wife of Sun God, who follows her husband like a shadow.
Gayathri	:	The creation of sage Viswamitra in the form of Chandas. Recited during Sandyavandanam daily.
Lalitha	:	Name of Goddess Parameswari. Very subtle body.
Lavanya	:	Beuatiful lady.
Kalyani	:	Blessed with good yeoman.
Kameswari	:	Goddess Parameswari who fulfills the desires of devotees.
Madhavi	:	Wife of Lord Madhava (Vishnu)
Mythili	:	Daughter of Janaka (King of Mithila).
Prasunapriya	:	Who loves flowers.
Padmaja	:	Born in lotus flower.
Padmini	:	Born in lotus pond.
Poornima	:	Full moon night.
Ramya	:	Beautiful.
Rekha	:	Part of moon (famous film star)
Sakuntala	:	Daughter of Menaka (married to king Bharata)
Sailaja	:	Daughter of king Himavantha (married to Lord Siva)
Sarita	:	River which flows.
Sirisha	:	A flower.
Shilpa	:	Art piece (Sculpture)
Sindhurika	:	Sindhur put on fore head by married ladies.
Sudha	:	Nector.
Sumana	:	A flower.
Sowmya	:	Girl with good manners.
Suneetha	:	Girl with morals.
Tripura Sundari	:	Goddess Parameswari.
Vani	:	Goddess of wisdom (Wife of Brahman)
Visalakshi	:	Lady with beautiful eyes.

School / College you studied – Important people associated

The interview can start with the place where you had your school / college education. Doon school / Bharatiya Vidyabhavan / IIT / IISC / Madras Presidency College / Shantiniketan / Roorkee / BHU / Aligarh Muslim University etc.

The questions related to the important personalities associated with the institutions can be leading the mood of the interview. Personalities like Rajiv Gandhi who was student of Doon College are to be narrated if you are from Doon School. Importance, history of institution, popularity, centre for excellence, teaching methods, autonomy, governing body are important.

Last Names

Last Names like Sastri, Sarma, Varma, Dwivedi, Trivedi, Chaturvedi are to be told of its importance.

Dwivedi : Who is proficient in two Vedas.

Trivedi : Proficient in three Vedas.

Chaturvedi : Proficient in four Vedas.

Then the immediate supplementary will be. Name the four Vedas? – Rig Veda, Yajur Veda, Sama Veda and Adharvana Veda. Traditional names like Sastri are popular in Brahmin communities of A.P. and U.P. Supplementary can be whether Lal Bahadur Sastri denotes his caste. Reply is no. 'Sastri' is title conferred on Lal Bahadur. Some of the caste names are to be explained in this manner.

Peculiar Names

Committee will be curious to know the meaning of peculiar names. For example :

Abbasi, Abhayankar, Ambarasu, Bagchee, Bhudev, Aswini, Subhendru, Ardrendru, Sekhar, Sukh Deep, Ambadas, Satyabrata, Alakananda, Beerbal, Arjun Bai.

Candidates should be able to narrate the peculiar circumstances under which he was named after that particular personality – legendary, historical, freedom fighter etc.

Popular Film Star Names

Dharmendra, Rekha, Bhanumathi, Amitab etc.

Simply mentioning that his parents are fans to particular star will not suffice. He shall explain how the star won applause from the public. Their popularity among the public is most important. Knowledge about the film personality, will lead to supplementaries. The history of film industry, annual releases in Hindi are to be kept in mind. If the candidate is from South the question of N.T. Rama Rao, Annadurai, Karunanidhi, Jayalalitha and Chiranjeevi will definitely emerge. Similarly film personalities who are members of Rajya Sabha and Lok Sabha in large numbers during the decade 2000-2010 can be a supplementary. Failure of Chiranjeevi in Andhra and success of N.T. Rama Rao are to be reasoned out. **Let the beginning be an upstart and not a Road block.**

Associated Names

Supplementary questions lead to names associated with your name.

Subbalakshmi : Can you tell us about a prominent personality of your name sake?

Ans : Bharata Ratna Dr. M.S. Subbalakshmi is an exponent of Karnatak Classical Music.

Rekha : Prominent Hindi Film Star associated with Amitabachan!

Sakunthala : The famous Maha Bharata Heroine who had love marriage with Prince Dushyantha and gave birth to Bharata.

Mythili : The daughter of Janaka, Seeta, named after the kingdom – Mithila.

Kalidas : Famous Sanskrit poet author of Abhijnana Sakunthala – play.

Pranab Kumar : Finance Minister in Dr. Manmohan Singh's Cabinet.

Parthasaradhi : Lord Krishna, Charioteer to Arjuna (Partha) and exponent of Bhagavadgeetha.

Bipinchandra : Famous freedom fighter – (Lal, pal, bal, trio freedom fighters).

Questions Related to Academic Qualifications

During the initial round of interview the first or second question will be on your qualifications.Relationship between unrelated subjects are to be justified.

Ex. M.Sc., B.L: Natuaral curiocity will be why you have choosen law after M.Sc. If you are not practing lawyer then the committee will ask why you have acquired law degree. The combination of electronics and mathematics; history and computers are to be related properly. Don't mention that it was not your choice and by accident you landed in to it.

At least fundamentals of the subject you have mentioned should be known by you. A person who did law two years back when

questioned was unable to even answer the fundamentals of constitution. Finally it was construed that he acquired it from a bogus university.

Post–Graduate diploma in Public Relations / Journalism / Astrology / Translation / Computer Sciences etc are additional qualifications. If they are acquired through distance education, the definite question will be whether you feel distance education mode is better than traditional.

Don't get confused. No body will question you, even if you answer either way. But, the reasoning shall be with supported concrete examples. It can be that "I am an employee and cannot afford going to evening classes / regular classes. Study material provided by distance education centres, classes, workshops, radio lessons and assignments helped me". Hard work is the main force. Journalism Diploma holders have to remember names of editors, News papers' circulation, regional language press etc.

Investigative Journalism, Yellow Journalism, district editions etc will be supplementary questions. Role of management in editorial policy, proprietors of daily newspapers controlling politics are to be explained in proper perspective. Negative approach is to be avoided. Blackmail methods adopted by Journalists can be explained. Be thorough with the subject.

A person acquired more than 25 degrees / diplomas and his bio data contains particulars of them. It is positive as well as negative sign. Be prepared for valley of questions. Fundamental knowledge of your basic degree is more important. Ex. Geology, Organic Chemistry, Electronics etc. If you are a student of literature - English / Hindi / Telugu/ Tamil you shall know the literary movements, prominent poets, their works and their popularity. Comparison between old and modern literature can be a question.

Don't mention simply the names like – Thulasi Das, Sura Das (Hindi), Shakespeare, Milton, Byron, Arnold (English); Nannayya, Thikkana, Pothana (Telugu); Subramanya Bharati, Vallattol (Tamil) as your favorite authors. Supplementary will definitely be about their works. If you mention Thulasi Das – tell about his Ramayana, its popularity in Hindi literature and the lucid style. If you have mentioned about Shakespeare tell about Macbeth, Othello and King Lear as his plays. The pioneering role played by Kavithraya poets in Telugu from 11th Century onwards is to be traced. Claim of Tamilians about Bharati and Vallattol is to explained in detail.

Don't mention that **"I don't know any more about the poets". "I did not study in detail" can be an answer. One candidate mentioned that he studied only the syllabus part for examinations.** Mere scoring of marks in the optional is not the criteria, learn more about the subject. Don't bluff as if you know everything on the subject. Instead of giving a wrong reply, excuse your self with – "I don't remember Sir". The committee tries to help you in familiarizing yourself with the subject and will ask questions based on the information provided by you in the proforma. Know more about modern researchers as well as current events on the subjects. Jnanpeeth Award winners of the Language is a common question. Not only the names but the works are to the remembered.

Ex: Viswanatha Satyanarayana – Ramayana Kalpavruksham. (Telugu) - 1970

Dr. C. Narayana Reddy - Viswambara. (Telugu) - 1989

Questions on Education / Experience

- Why you have selected the particular college for degree / PG?
- What type of a student you are? (Sober etc.)
- Can you mention one memorable incident at the college?
- You are a science graduate / arts? Why you have applied for this job?
- Can you mention your extra curricular activities?
- Were you in-charge of any position in the college like – NCC leader / NSS leader / Cultural president / Union President.
- How did your internship help you?
- What is your percentage in degree / PG?
- Did you face any difficulties in the college?

These type of questions are most common. The interviewer is interested to know your temperament / aptitude / leadership qualities. They know that without any formal training no fresher can do well in the job.

Best Answers can be -

On Choice of Science / Arts subjects :

- "I am really interested in the subject. I have taken it not because it is easy".

If you have changed from sciences to arts – be prepared to give reasons. But that will lead to several supplementaries. Keep the answer brief and be positive.

Regarding percentage of marks –

Interviewer would like to see your Marks sheets. (explain reasons for less percentage in one or two subjects).

Memorable Experience : Focus them on career oriented points. Your liking towards a particular professor / lecturer. Any strike, agitation that took place during your studies. The discipline in the college etc. But make sure that your answer reflects your mind set.

Extra curricular activities: The question can be "why you have not participated actively in extra curricular activities?"

Ans : "Sir, I spent most of my time concentrating on studies and examinations. I wish I should have participated more in cultural activities. I am interested in acting in stage plays, social work / literary activities. But, my Professors sincerely advised me to increase my grade. I wanted to get rank in the college / university."

Take care in answering. If you claim more about extra curricular activities, interviewer will definitely ask about your studies. Anything you have done to demonstrate your leadership skills will be appreciated.

Some **tough questions** at this juncture :

- Tell us about your failure.
- How you got first rank.
- Last mistake you have done
- Any project work undertaken.
- Have you failed in your goal.
- Solving any problem.
- Tough time with your teacher / friend.
- Too much work to do.
- Are you bored with examinations.

The answers must be coherent and specific. It is a **launching pad for success** and similarly more detailed questions. So, be careful.

Answer to the point : When the question is replied, look into the eyes of interviewer and listen to the next question. Answer to the point. If you are asked about specific facts, **don't provide entire information you have. Answer only the facts he asked for.**

It shall be direct reply. Longish answers will not fit in. Don't be under the impression that your quick answer to the question will be appreciated. Take a short pause after the question and give a suitable answer. Employees look for enthusiasm, vigour, confidence and above all dependability.

Open ended questions :

They are like double edged sword. It is difficult to answer. But be careful.

- Why you have opted for sciences in degree?
- How your friend describes you?

- Why do you want to join us?
- What are your goals?
- How do you feel if you are not seleted?
- What are your strengths ?
- What are your long range plans?
- Who is your role model?
- How you will perform on the job?
- Who really you are made of?
- Your education and job experience?

These type of questions are most common and the replies must be factual and constructive. It needs lot of preparation.

Questions as a team leader

What is your aim for accomplishment in life?

- What type of supervisor you like?
- A – B – C – D (Autocratic, Beaurocratic, Cooperative, Democratic) - Bosses
- Do you prefer to work in a team or you want to lead?
- How do you manage conflicts in the team?
- What requires for a change in your personality?
- Do you want to play safe?
- Are you a trouble shooter?
- What is the opinion about you from your friends / peers?
- If you have tug of war with your boss – what will you do?
- How you will act under stress?

Remember

The employer expects – honesty, confidence and enthusiasm. Don't give negative information about you. Let him know that you are comfortable in a team. He should know that you are a loyalist. Extra curricular activities connected with the job are to be told.

Know your Job : Through different sources – Internet, officers working in the institute, annual reports and friends learn more about the organization, before interview. information about the Head quarters, hierarchy, Regional offices, funding agencies. Main thrust of the organization, Financial station, organizational structure, promotional avenues, HRD structure are to be ascertained.

Normal questions will be :

- Do you know your duties in the job?
- Are you suitable for the Job?
- Can you work in for flung areas of North East / J & K.

- Who is the CMD / Director / Commissioner / EO?
- Where are the Regional offices located?
- Attached offices to the main office?
- Whether it is a public sector undertaking?
- What are the funding agencies?
- Present financial status of the organization?
- What is the main objective?

If it is an organization for AIDS control, Adult literacy and it involves public cooperation how do you go about it?)

- Whether your qualifications suit for the job?
- Training you have undergone related to the Job?
- Specialization you have done for the Job?
- Promotional Avenues of the organization?
- Prominent people working / worked in the organization.
- Recent News about the organisation?
- Corrupt practices if any? How do you rectify them?
- Difficulties in the Job?
- Why do you like the Job?
- Will you be leaving the Job for better opportunities?
- Foreign tours are expected. Are you prepared?
- Touring Job? Are you ready?
- Odd hour duties - are you mentally prepared?

These type of questions are area specific and your answer should not be "yes or no" type. Give reasons for like or dislike.

Questions on your Main subject : Depending on your graduation / post graduation subject – science / arts / commerce / Engineering, one of the member will be questioning you about the subject. In-depth interview to answer your knowledge on the subject will be conducted. This is the main part of the interview, where you can show your metal. Latest researches on the subject are to be covered in the replies. Nobel prize winners and prominent awards announced in the field are most important. If the subjects of your graduation and post-graduation are different, coherent reasons for the same is to be mentioned. **"I did not get college seat of my choice" - will not be liked.**

Names of the JournalS/ Magazines available on the subject are to be collected and recent papers published are to be mentioned besides the Editorial Board. Replies not exceeding two to three minutes will be ideal. **Do not enter into argument that your view point is only correct. "As fAr as my knowledge goes" – is the best way to put forth your view.**

The other member including chairman will be observing your way of replies, your confidence level, authority on the subject, communication skills, body language/ over action, argumentative style, over simplicity, shyness. Lack of coherence in your speech is observed by the committee as a whole. If you do not know the full answer you can admit your ignorance instead of explaining it more and creating a bad impression. You can reply partly and excuse yourself. If you do not know the answer admit that I am not aware. Replies supplemented by facts and figures / years / names will impress the Board. If you are not able to understand the question you can ask the member to repeat / rephrase the question. Commission will never feel it as bad. Do not say that the question is out of syllabus. **For personal / oral interviews there is no syllabus. Any thing on the face of the earth can be questioned.** The Board has all sympathy for the candidate and will help him to come out of his web. They may cross examine you and yet times be aggressive in questioning. Reply politely and honestly. It will pay.

Questions on optionals :

Definitely there will be a question on your optional subjects : History / Sociology / Telugu / Tamil etc. Be confident to answer. History is a vast subject and the syllabus you have studied is to be remembered. Questions on socio economic conditions and the impact of Moghul period are common. Supplementary questions also will follow. If you have science subjects, have updated knowledge.

Reading the subject for examinations is different. But get thoroughly prepared for the personal interview. The question about Nobel Prize winners of the particular subject, their contributions, the country to which they belong, year he won Nobel Prize are important to remember.

The question **why you have chosen the optional is also common. Do not reply that getting score in the subject is easy.** If your graduation and post graduation are in science / arts / engineering / medicine / Business Administration and the optional chosen and not related you have to explain in detail about reason for selecting the option.

Questions about your State: Knowledge about your native place. Native district and the Native state are expected. Common questions :

(1) What for is your village known for.
(2) Prominent persons from the village.
(3) Advantages and disadvantages in studying at a village.
(4) Demography and social conditions of the village.
(5) Communication facilities available.
(6) Medical facilities available.
(7) Irrigation facilities

(8) Profession of your father

(9) Temples / Tourist places at the place.

(10) What kind of social activities you will take up in your village after getting a decent job.

The replies to these questions are to be supplemented with concrete examples and dates about the place. **Do not reply that "I hardly stayed in my village".** Collect information about your village though you have not stayed there. Ancestral heritage is to be Told. Be proud that you are from a village. The commitment to your village and your ambition to uplift communication, medical facilities of the village are to be narrated.

Supplimentaries can be on Rural Vs Urban Population, migration to cities, Panchayat Raj system, faction politics, democracy at gross root level, and empowerment of woman, caste system. Conditions of Dalits, Atrocities by land lords / upper castes are points for discussion. The reply shall be in two to three sentences followed by certain data relevant to the answer. **If you are giving percentages be sure it correlates with the facts at a glance.**

State: Importance of your state : Population, Demographic figures, Rivers, Politicians, Political Parties, Assembly constituencies, Temples / Tourist places are common. Advantages and disadvantages of smaller states, reorganization, formation of smaller states, Telangana and Vidharbha agitations, first linguistic state formation in 1953 (Andhra State) are points to be remembered.

Contribution of your state at National level in various fields – political, economical, Industrial aspects are to be highlighted. Role of Regional parties, emergence of United Front Government are to be discussed. States like UP, Maharashtra, Gujarat, Tamil Nadu, Andhra Pradesh have specialties to be mentioned. Jammu and Kashmir has special status. Smaller states like Puducherry, Goa have special problems. Andaman and Nicobar Islands have special status.

Administrative set up in Union Territories like Chandigarh is peculiar, They are directly under the control of Ministry of Home affairs in day to day administration.

Order of Preference given by the candidates in civil services is point for discussion. Besides home state preference the second preference will be questioned if it is not a neighboring state.

Candidate shall go through Manorama year book and collect population, education, industrial figures of the state and add on information for supplimentaries. Publication division of Ministry of

Information and Broadcasting, Govt. of India Publishes Year book which contain lot of information containing basic material about the states. Candidates shall go through the book and jot down points for ready reference. If a candidate is from UP / Uttarakhand he shall be able to tell about importance of Mussorie and Dehradun. Mussorie is the place where IAS officers are trained at Lalbahadur Sastri Academy. It is a training place for all Civil Servants. Similarly Dehradun is the training place for Indian Forest Service Officers. Sardar Vallabhai Patel National Police Academy for IPS officers is at Hyderabad. Nagpur is the centre for Indian Revenue Officers (Income Tax etc.) One shall be clear about these National Academies in the country.

District

Similar Questions on the native district are also expected. If the district has a river / mountain / temple / Tourist place / Industry / Political figure do not forget to add. Tamil Nadu and other Southern states are full of Temples and temple architecture. Madurai, Mahabalipuram, Kanchi, Kanyakumari. Tiruvannamalai, Tiruttani, Kurtalam, Tenkasi, Kumbakonam, Tirupati, Mantralayam, Udipi, Dharmasthala, Mysore - the famous dieties and festival seasons are important to mention besides tourist facilities available. Industrial infrastructure available in the district is to be told.

The prominent political personality from your district in the central cabinet and his contribution to National party are to be mentioned. Poets/ artists of the area are to be remembered. Parliamentary / Assembly constituencies in the district and representatives of the area are to be mentioned.

Constituencies of Dr. Man Mohan Singh, Mr. Pranab Mukherjee, Chidambaram, Mayavati, Meera Kaur, Mamata Benerjee, Lalu Prasad Yadav etc. are to be rembered. If they belong to your native place mention for how many times they are representing that particular constituency. Film stars of the area and their debut film are to be remembered. The answer shall not be "yes / no" type. It shall be illustrative and imformative.

Supplementary can be how many districts are in your state and the economic conditions of the district. Prominent News paper / Journalists of the area, women in power are points for discussion.

Whether it is a backward district or industrially potential is to be mentioned. Do not forget to add cultural / historical importance of the District. Each district has its own specialties in various fields. The Panchayat Raj system in the district and its success are points for discussion.

Questions on General Knowledge

This is a tricky area. Candidates ability to group things, his knowledge about the worldly affairs are Judged in this segment.

Political Subjects

Democracy and its success or failure.

Coalition Governments.

Regional Parties.

UPA Govt. Vs NDA Govt.

Role of Presidents.

Prime Ministers of the Country, special mention about Dr. Manmohan Singh (2004-2009 and 2009 -)

His first term achievement / second term policies. Names of Prominent Lok Sabha Members and Rajya Sabha Members.

Current political situation.

Main news on the interview day and its repercussions.

— This is only a wish list but hundred more subjects can be added depending on the mood of the interview. **To set the mood of the interview the replies shall be creative and not imaginative.** Historical persopective is to be added. Socio economic conditions during the period are to be mentioned. Rule of Jawaharlal Nehru and Nehruvian Policies during plan period are to be remembered. Janata Party rule, excess of emergency period are to be analyzed.

Social Aspects: Bills presented recently in Parliament / Pending Bills. Your views on the bill or your analytical view.

- Reservation Bill for women in Parliament.
- New Education Policy.
- Naxalism
- Kashmir Policy
- North East Policy of Government
- Government Programmes – Central and State, NREGP, Indira Kranti, AIDS Control etc.
- Constitutional amendments for social development.
- Constitutional amendments for Panchayat Raj

Total Employees

Normally a question is leveled against the candidate who is already working in an office / organization. A typical example is given :

A candidate appeared for the selection of Station Director post in All India Radio at UPSC. He is already working in the

organization for the last 15 yrs. The Chairman of the Board asked a similar question :
How many people are working in All India Radio?
(The Director General AIR was also a Member and Present)
Candidate: Sir, If my DG Permits - I will say : 'very few people are working in All India Radio. If you rephrase It – How many people are employed, I have an answer"
Everyone in the Board appreciated his ready wit. Candidate knew the exact number of employees working say 14,000 – But it will lead to several supplementaries like how many engineer, how many programmers etc.
To avoid all such complications candidate has chosen the reply.

But be sure to collect the information about the number of employees working. The hierarchy and who is reporting to whom and nature of your Job.

International Issues: This is a provocative area. Most probable questions include:

- Decisions of SAARC countries.
- Meetings of Common wealth countries.
- NAM summits – Indian Participation
- UNO Conferences
- Recent visits of foreign dignitaries to India.
- Visit of PM / President to foreign countries.
- Indo – China Border issue.
- Indo – Pak relations
- Status of Dalialama
- Indo – Srilankan ties
- Indo – Nepal friendship
- Policies of Barrack Obama.

All the questions related to International ties are to be answered, if you are aware of the latest developments. Any pacts signed by both the countries, cultural agreements are to be highlighted. Indo-Pak border issue is a burning topic. Role of Bhutto, Zia-ul-Haq, Benazir Bhutto, Gen Musharraf in Indo Pak ties is to be understood before you answer. If you are not sure tell the Board that you are not aware of the recent events on the subject. But International issues are most commonly discussed subjects in personal interviews. Study them carefully and remember names of important personalities of each country.

In a hurry to reply do not mix personalities with one country to the other. General information about neighboring countries is to be updated by reading current affairs. It is suggested that spot light of All India Radio broadcast at 9.15 pm every day gives lot of information on Government topics. The scripts of spot light are available with AIR New Delhi (DG News). Search *www.airnews.co.in.*

Questions on Literature : The candidates' optional language will form a major part of the personal interview. The subject expert who is well versed in the language – Hindi, Urdu, Tamil, Telugu, Kannada, Malayalam and other 14 Regional languages will be eliciting information about the literary knowledge of the candidate.

Probable Questions :

- Prominent authors of the language.
- Literary movements in 20th Century.
- Jnanpeeth Award winners.
- Ancient writers / poets.
- Modern Trends.
- Dalit Movement
- Women writers of the area.
- Recent Sahitya Academy Award winners.
- Prominent writings during 15th/ 16th / 20th century.
- Contemporary writers.
- Books you like / Read
- Narrate few lines of your choice from any poet.
- Have you written any articles / books.
- Your favourite writers.
- Short story / novel / poetry writers.
- Prominent Daily News papers in your language.
- Literary Magazines.

Your knowledge about the language and literature shall be exhaustive. **Do not give the reply "I don't remember or I have no idea".** That does not mean you reply what ever you know. Literature is a vast subject and **you direct the interview in your favour.** Mention that "I prefer modern literature / fiction/ poetry" – instead of vague replies. **Be specific about what you know and what you do not know.** Inform the Board about your strengths. Do not expose your weakness.

General Questions:

- Questions about your music knowledge.
- Sports / games you play.
- Hobbies, reading / viewing films and cooking are general impressions, be specific.

- Languages you know (other than mother tongue)
- Tourist places / temples you visited.
- Diplomas / degrees you have obtained.
- Research work you have done.
- Cine stars you like – Male and Female. Instead of replying Amitab Bachan and Iswarya Rai as favourites mention about their peculiarities / films you have seen.
- Sport stars you like (other than cricket)
- Cricketers you like (their game history)
- Your Teachers at Primary school / college.
- TV Channels mostly you watch.
- Your rating of news channels
- Your knowledge about political parties
- Election commission of India
- Democratic set up – its failures
- Unrest in youth
- Unemployment problem.
- Constitutional provisions.
- Right to information Act.

This is the final round where your imagination and competency are Judged. Simple replies will not do. Add colour to your answer. Qualify the answer. The answer can be :

Tourist places I visited include Kanchipuram in South. It is known for the diety Kanchi Kamakshi and famous Varadaaraja Temple. Siva Kanchi and Vishnu Kanchi are popular. His holiness Sri Audi Sankara established Kanchi Kamakoti Peetham. Sri Jayendra Saraswati Swamigal is the main Pontiff at Present. This will give an outlook about your ability to learn things.

Question on Better opportunities

Candidate is working and has opted for better opportunities.

The scenario can be :

Present Post:	***Post being Interviewed***
Private Job	Govt. Job
State Govt. Job	Higher pay scale / state / central
Central Govt. Job	Higher pay scale (Central)
Department not connected with public	Public Department

Lower Cadre	Higher Cadre
Group B Post State / Central	Group 'A' Post / State / Central
Civil Services Group A	Better Civil Services like IAS and IPS
Public Sector	Private Sector
Public Sector	State / Central Govt.
Placement Outside Native State	In Naitve State
Job unconnected with his qualifications	Suited for his qualifications
Spouse working in different service	To work together with the spouse in same dept.
No promotion	Promotional avenues
No pension	Pensionable Job
Banking Services	Regular Service
Night duties	Regular Duties

Many more choices are probable. The interview board likes to know why you have opted for the change. Keep your mind very clear. 'I get more salary, 'I will get a posting in my native state', Promotion chances are more" are the regular replies.

"I want to serve the public, I like the Job" - are spicy, be clear about your objective. Reasoning and understanding is more important. Aim at higher goals. Set the priorities in your mind spelt out clearly. You have to face valley of questions. Answer them carefully. **If you falter at any stage due to over enthusiasm you will be caught unaware.** My parents / teachers / friends advised me to opt for the new Job is not expected.

Probable Questions

- Why you want to have a change?
- What are your main duties at present?
- Presently whom do you report to?
- How many years of service you have put in?
- Are you happy?
- Why you have Joined Job unconnected with you.
- Is it through state public service commission?
- Your interaction with public.
- How your previous experience suit the new job.
- Present emoluments.
- Youl prefer Govt. Job since it is secure?
- Do you opt out if pension benefits are not there?
- Are you ready to work in rural areas?

- Why you are leaving public sector?
- Why do you apply for so many jobs?
- Your qualification is different from the Job requirement
- What are the main duties of the Job you are being interviewed.
- Your spouse is in different department. Do you want to change?
- Whether your motive is to serve public.
- If you are given full powers as District Head what will be your priority.
- If you are given powers of CM / PM what is your priority.
- Are you prepared to work in North East / J & K.
- Are you ready to work at difficult stations.
- Do you prefer to be in middle level management or in CEO seat?

Replies to all the above questions are not structured. Basing on the situation and your aptitude you can frame the replies. Be honest. **Nothing pays than being honest.** Lighter vein questions are to be answered with genuineness. No hoodwinking by replying – "I want to serve the county. I am not for higher emoluments" - may not click. Be honest.

Anecdotes

Board members would like to know about the candidates' previous experience and his achievements. Two anecdotes are worth mentioning.

A candidate from Andhra Pradesh worked as conductor in Road Transport Corporation for 3 years. He obtained post graduate degree and qualified himself for civil services in 2010. The member was curious to know about his past.
Question : How do you utilize your previous experience as conductor for 3 years when you become a district administrator.
Reply: Sir, I worked hard to get post graduate degree through Distance Education. RTC Bus is a mini state with mini culture. It represents people from all strata - Middle class, lower class and down trodden. They discuss about day to day problems, politics, hike in prices and everything. They argue with emotion during the short time available. It is a real feed back. As Govt. officer at the helm of affairs in the district I convert their ambitions into reality.
To sight an example, one evening while I was conducting the Bus to the district Head quarters, an women from Rural areas visiting the town for delivery had sudden labour pains.

Immediately I requested the driver to take the bus quickly to a nearby Government Hospital. The woman delivered within minutes. To the surprise of all there hospital nurse said that she does not have a safety blade to cut the umbilical chord of the child.

What a shame? As District Collector I shall give priority to such small things and provide minimum requirements in a Government Hospital"

With this answer the board was happy. His attitude towards poor, his grasp over the subject, his analytical approach, his comparison of a bus as mini state were well taken. The strong realities at ground level are well presented. The reply is well received.

Another candidate during 2010 civil services interviews told that he worked as Auto rickshaw driver in Andhra for 2 years. These two examples are two extremes but they cannot be over ruled. Hard work and studiousness pays.

Questions on Current Affairs

Probable questions – "what is important news to day.

(Lady Judge was appointed on that day to Supreme Court). Candidates who have not noticed it may fail to answer.

- Death of an intellectual.

Dining the month of April 2010 the business Guru Dr. C.K. Prahlad passed away. Number of articles / tributes appeared in all National Dailies about him.

Candidate shall be able to tell about C.K. contribution to Business world. His theory of pyramid on poverty is to be explained. Mere mention of his name may not help.

News in Parliament

Introduction of any bill and voting process.

Stand of opposition and ruling party on women's reservation bill.

Budget session – approval of Tax proposals.

- News from states (South, North, North East and J & K)

All the major news items are to be noted. On the day of the interview go through the major dailies (one or two). Read the Editorial page and remember main points.

Events during the month are important. Supreme Court rulings, Government orders issued in public interest, matters concerned to common man, price hike, inflation rate, GDP rate are main focus points for discussion.

Public opinion on major developments for and against Government is to be kept in mind. Remember recent appointments made to Raj Bhavans, Supreme Court, Election Commission, cabinet etc. Respectable Cabinet ministers are most important. Deaths of high dignitaries, visit of foreign dignitaries, National Games, Common wealth games, are points a candidate should recollect when questioned. He may not be interested in polictics, games etc. But he should remember important events in detail to be explained. **The ball is in your court play it with vigour and enthusiasm. You will definitely win.**

Tough Questions

You are faring well in the interview and suddenly a tough question is posed. **You end up in confusion, tongue – tied or give a stupid answer.** You think, you have lost the chance. Don't worry. It was a deliberate attempt. It is to gauge your reaction and to know your response. Career counselors advise the candidates to be calm. The tricky question during the interview is to make you confused and let unintelligible answer.

In such a situation take a pause (deep breath if necessary) for a while and give suitable reply. Frame appropriate response. You can ask the question to be repeated. It you have not understood the question ask to explain. Common questions expected at interviews are to be guessed. Prepare for such questions and frame answers.

Get the information about the company interviewing you either from website or from employees. Be prepared to answer. Common questions are –

(I) – why do you want to join this company?

Answer : I am lucky to be absorbed in a great organization. (Sounds flattery and insincerity and artificial.)

(B) Professional response : I know the company through my relatives / friends / well wishers. The training facilities / career opportunities for promotion are good. I like the firm's future plans in the next few years. I aspire to be a participant in the growth.

(II) What are your strengths and weakness?

(Very tricky you can talk about your strengths, but difficult to explain weakness.)

Answer: My educational qualifications / research work / experience are best suited for the post. I have communication skills to market the products.

Regarding my weakness I do not think I may fail? During the initial month with the guidance of my senior colleagues I am sure I will be successful.

(III) Tell us about yourself?

Ans: I did my post graduation from an established Institution like IIT / JNU / Delhi University / Madras University.

I have scored I class marks in Sciences / Arts / Engineering. I have put in 3 year service at a reputed company.

- This is a big list. Throw open your academic qualifications. Don't try to tell about your studies, difficulties unless they are uncommon. Tell about your achievements.

Honest and Brief Answer without Adulation is Required

If you are a fresher talk about your skills.

Your communication skills are Judged during the response.

(IV) What is your career goal?

Answer: Sir, It is difficult to explain – however I will attempt. In the next five years I want to settle down in life, get married. With regard to my goal I want to be a middle level manager. I want to pursue research work. God has to give me opportunity.

(This answer requires prior thinking and clear cut goal. Some research on your career growth in the organization is needed. It depends upon the post you applied for. Be careful. Don't make remarks with over enthusiasm. This question is meant to know your enthusiasm level. They will gauge your specific goals and your competency)

(V) Can you tell us about a tough situation you Landed?

Ans. Fresher : So far the opportunity to take such situation has not come.

2 to 3 yrs. Experienced: I will narrate my humble contribution to the organization I am serving. The company was in doldrums. Targets are given. As a middle level manager I encouraged my colleagues to work hard and get better results. By God's grace and with the guidance of my senior officer our team achieved the targets during quarter 4.

Tell me about yourself

This is the favorite question by an experienced interviewer. It gives him the opportunity to know about the candidate, his reactions and body language. The question can be asked by an unprofessional interviewer just to extract information. Better to be prepared for such a question. Develop the answer and rehearse it.

The interviewer wants to feel good about you. The duty of the candidate is to let him does just that?

> **Ron Fry in his book "Your first Interview" mentions:**
> **"The hiring manager wants you to make him feel confident that hiring you will be a god decision. Your answer to this question should be targeted to do just that".**

While preparing the answer the following points are to be kept in mind :

- Your key achievements
- Area of knowledge
- Professional skills
- Rich personality
- Things you can do best.

This introduction shall give your experience suited to the requirements of the position. The summary shall be logically sequenced. It shall be able to focus your skills in 250 to 300 words and not exceeding 2 mts. Sequence will be –

Brief introduction, main accomplishments, your strengths and importance of this to employer. Reharse it at home.

Write your answer and rephrase it. It shall sound natural and conversational. All the key points are to be emphasized. Look for supplementary questions after your reply. After finishing your reply you shall have lot more to add.

Don't miss the opportunity to sell yourself. The fact that you have been called for the interview has given a chance to sell yourself. Interviewer wants a best person for the job. Keep it in mind.

(VI) Question: Hypothetical: you are the CEO of public sector BHEL. The company has run into loses? You have 6 months to set it right. What you will do.

Ans.: No clear cut response can be elucidated. The question is to answer your problem solving skills and your management activities in handling difficult situations. The response shall be an honest account of a past experience if you are working. If you are a fresher try to build a good response. Phase out the reply in two phases. Point I, Point II – like that the reply can be given. Talk about short term measures – 6 to 10 months – long term measures – 1 to 5 years.

If a candidate is well prepared for such questions there is no need to be panicky. Rehearse yourselves for such questions. Think of two alternatives. Your answers are to be brief and to the point. Relate it to the job and project yourself in a positive light.

Body language should not betray your un-preparedness and confusion. It shall exude professional outlook and full confidence. **If you are well prepared for such situations you have won half the battle.**

(VII) Take initiative: Take the initiative in providing useful information for the interviewer in order to evaluate your suitability for the position. Don't give yes / no answers. Answer briefly and support it with relevant evidence from past experience. Interviewer is not interested to listen to long and comprehensive replies.

Don't recite the answers as if you are prepared. You should memorize the ideas and answer in a natural and spontaneous way.

Answer positively even if your answer is negative, offer clear and positive explanations. Be honest and sincere about your weakness or short comings and turn it into positive. Be careful in using the words – 'sure, obviously, of course, no problem, as you know – "It gives a feeling of arrogance. Positive replies can be – "I believe that … I do not see a major problem in it." Avoid the phrases – To be frank, to be honest, "It gives an impression that you are not honest in your previous replies.

Some Real Happenings at Interviews

The worst a candidate can expect in an interview unfavourable to him is–

- Ill suited dress. An young man extremely nervous in the interview hall fumbled. His suit jacket opened. His immediate reaction was – "sorry sir, this is my father's wedding suit" – everyone laughed at his innocence.
- Another candidate followed the advice of his senior friend. Relax– Relax. No answer for few minutes even after the question was repeated.
- Profuse sweating during the interview. Stay calm. Never move your eyes from the interviewer. Take few seconds to compose and reply.
- It is only a situation created to know your reactions under a pressure. The interviewer has no agenda to defeat you.
- It is only a test to observe whether you will become depressed, get confused under stress when the interview becomes difficult.

- It is important to keep your voice at a medium pitch. The speed in answering, the communication skills are noticed. Don't feel sorry and say 'sorry' for each and every question / answer.

First impression is the best impression

Your dress, politeness, demeanor, communication skills are the best to show at the time of interview. For the first time you are encountering a new person / persons. They have very high stake on you. They are going to employ you for 25 yrs. are more. So try to show you best. This is the only time when you can dress yourself to impress them. **Interview is a game. Play it well as per rules of the game.**

Telephone Interviews

Most of the software companies do the screening through telephone interviews. At the given fixed time the call materializes and the candidate is interviewed for about 20 mts depending on the mood. Candidates are screened to shortlist. The interview will be qualitative. Your enthusiasms for the new position, emotional distrubance, articulation at the time of replies, nervousness are counted. Compared to personal interview this is in a way better since your mannerisms and body language are not noticed.

Do's and Don'ts in an interview

Do's

- Come at least 20 mts. early.
- Enter the room politely
- Address the interviewer with Good Morning / Afternoon.
- Shake hands properly – if he / she offer.
- Take your seat with permission.
- Maintain good eye contact.
- Don't cut short the question.
- Take a pause to answer.
- Ask for clarification, in case of any doubt.
- Be positive
- Stress your qualification.
- Inform your readiness to join duties.

Don'ts

Poor grooming, showing up late, inappropriate dress.

- Smoke ½ hr before. (You may smell)
- Chew anything
- Apologize for less experience

- Ask about pay and perks unless necessary.
- Handle items on the table of interviewer
- Discuss personal problems
- Tell about other jobs you did not get.
- Criticize earlier employers.
- Provide information about not factual
- An answer that simply does not answer the question.
- Lack of knowledge about the company / Job
- Dishonesty
- Lack of enthusiasm / interest
- Disparity in your resume

Hobbies : One Real Situation :

Mr. Prakash mentioned in his C.V. Cricket and reading as his hobbies.

The Chairman asked him about the books he has read during the last 2 months. The answer was "Sir, I was preparing for the personal interview". He was an economics postgraduate. Then the question was what Books you read for interview. The answer was not encouraging. He said Competition success, Civil service chronicle. Another member asked him about 'Yojana'. The answer was planning. He does not know that a monthly - called Yojana is published in English and other languages.

The second aspect was about cricket.

"whether you have played for your College/ University?

Answer : No sir, in my town only during summer holidays, I played with my friends for few hours.

Next question : Who is your favourite Cricketer?

Answer : After a big pause of 1mt. Mr. Patoudi.

(The age of the candidate is less than 30yrs. Patoudi's innings were in 70's. So the Answer did not suit.)

So, be careful in writing the column of hobbies.

Prepare well for an answer

First impression

Walter Vieira, who has spent 15 years as a corporate executive in his book Job Interviews mentions his views on first impression. "The battle is half way one with a good start.... The clarity, tone and strength with which you speak will also determine the impression you make on the interviewer.... Do a quick check on yourself.

- Do you speak so softly that interviewer cannot hear you or have to strain to hear? They may ask you to repeat a few times and after that either will give up or cease to care.
- Do you mumble or speak too fast.
- Do you vary your tone to make hearing pleasant?"

Think about these points and practice your way of replying.

Prof. P. Murali, Former Vice Chancellor, S.V. University, Tirupati

Expresses his views on the mood of the Interviewer.

"Physical appearance creates an impression about a person to some extent. It has a little role while selecting a candidate. The candidate should have three qualities.· Patience in listening to other's views; Clarity in communicating his own views and ·Pleasing manners while interacting with others. The minimum time taken to judge a candidate is 10 to 15 mts. On the part of the interviewer he should remove the tension in the interviewee by asking his hobbies, future plans etc. The success in answering the first two questions increases the confidence level to face the rest of the interview."

Communication Skills

Mr. C. Ramakant Sarma, PR consultant & HRD trainer in an article in Employment news has diagnosed number of problems faced by students in communication :

1. "Some students write well, but they are not able to express themselves orally.
2. Some speak fluently but cannot write without grammatical errors.
3. Some are comfortable in speaking among themselves in a small group, but are not comfortable facing the audience.
4. Some have problems with their body language and use inappropriate gestures while interacting with others. Some find it difficult to maintain eye contact. Some are always misunderstood".

Students face problems in group communication also: it includes

- Fear of expressing certain views.
- Lack of exposure and practice.

- Lack of fluency and confidence.
- Lack of interpersonal and group skills.

Similarly they have problems in writing skills. Communication in writing includes accuracy, appropriateness, attractiveness, avoidance of ambiguity. Correctness, clarity, consistency and concreteness are important. Students are required to have reading skills, speaking skills, listening skills and conversational skills.

People using positive language are effective communicators. Their message, written or oral would be polite, pleasant, practical, persuasive and powerful. Positive language creates a positive impact on the receiver and helps in attaining the goal. Avoid using negative words. Communication flows like a river. Communication is the life line of management and is vital for good management.

Postmortem of Interview

Most of the time candidates feel that he has done the personal interview very well. But it is not correct. You should look at the other side of the coin. The interviewer shall feel happy about your performance. Better the candidate himself reviews his performance after the interview is over. After getting back home, in a cool and calm atmosphere, analyze what you have told from the beginning to the end.

Check list for Review

- Number of questions asked.
- No. of replies with full satisfaction.
- No. of wrong replies.
- No. of incomplete replies.
- Reaction of members / Chairman for the answers.
- Your problem in communicating in English.
- Whether the replies should have been much better.
- Any points to be remembered for next interview.

Make note of all these points in a diary for further reference. Improve your performance with rehearsals.

> **Walter Vieira says :**
>
> "A Man who has committed a mistake and does not correct it is committing another mistake... The only boundaries we have are in form. There are no obstacles in thought".
>
> Final decision in an interview is based on interviewer's perception and 'feel'. Finding and what the interviewee knows is relevant. This can be improved by developing greater objectivity.

Frequent Failures in Interviews

There may be an occasion where you have failed consequently for three times in personal interviews, even though you have good track record in college. Please sit for a moment coolly and do introspection. You will be able to know the reasons:

- Always it is not true that influential persons alone will get.
- Are you eligible for the post?
- How was your performance?
- What went wrong in the interview?
- Is it lack of communication?
- Plan for future interviews.
- Equip your self with better answers.
- Project your strengths.

Mr. A. K. Agarwala, President, Hindalco Industries limited observes:

"That the interview is only a means to prove the personality of the candidate and find out how well he would be fit in the new organization. At the most, interview is therefore an exploration and one can not be certain about the outcome..... The process of interview is an odyssey both for the interviewer and the candidate. Both must continue to remain on the part of learning and application".

Jamshed J Irani – Managing Director, TATA Steels Limited (TISCO) observes that he gives weightage to the following two characters of a candidate:

1. Persons having direct eye contact.
2. Answering with little smile and confidence

SWOT Analysis

Every individual has to know his strengths and weakness. SWOT analysis is not a complicated theory. It is a measurement of

S – Strength, W = Weakness, O = Opportunities; T = Threats.

It needs an honest look at yourself. Make clear assessment of all threats and opportunities in your chosen field – writer, lawyer, journalist, professor, engineer or doctor.

You may not be suitable for group working in a team. Then don't choose the job which involves a team. People with indication towards desk bound Jobs are suitable for corporate planners. Some people are balanced in thinking and can reach top positions, because they are very strong at thinking as well as implementation of their plans.

Look out for Right Opportunities

Opportunities on net are available. Naukari.com, Monster.com solicit CVs. This is a free service. Recruits approach them for candidates. With capacity of net, thousands of CVs can be easily accessed and right choice can be made. Campus interviews are the best for selections. It suits the company to select a raw graduate. For the candidate also he is assured of the job immediately after the course.

Applying for a job, appearing for personal interviews and getting selections are a long drawn process. Sometimes if luck favours you may come across an acquaintance in a very senior position of a company. He comes forward to help you after seeing your pleasing manners.

> ***A Real Situation :***
>
> *Mr. Saxena works for a five star Hotel at New Delhi in reception. The Chairman and Managing Director of an MNC came to the Hotel. Mr. Saxena attended on him for about 15 minutes and made him comfortable in VIP suit. The CMD pleased at the hospitality extended by Mr. Saxena gave his Business card and asked him to call for any help. After few weeks Mr. Saxena approached him and gave his CV. He requested him for any sales / Marketing position in the company. Luck smiled on him. On the recommendation of CMD of the company, HRD interviewed him and selected him as sales manager. Mr. Saxena later rose up to Regional Sales Manager and later became General Manager.*

Latest Interview Techniques

Video resumes are scrutinized and telephonic interviews are conducted. Asia Pacific institute of broadcast development (AIBD) Koulalampur, a broadcast organization recruited its Director through telephonic interview. During 2002, the post of Director, AIBD fell vacant when Mr. Dato Abdul Mohammad retired. Several senior officials from different countries and AIR & DD officials from India applied for the post. My candidature was short listed for interview. They have asked for my convenient time and land line phone number. HR manager from Recruiting agency has telephoned me and the interview took place for about 25 mts. The main thrust was about my experience in Radio for the last 3 decades. I did well. One Director from Japan broadcasting organization was selected.

Avaya- Global – connect has developed a software which enables companies to speed up interviews. The travel of the candidate to the interview place and costs to the company are reduced. For MNC companies recruiting candidates across the globe, this is an easy way. With the help of an interview voice response system the interview is conducted and entire proceedings are recorded and HR team will later analyze it.

www.bravenewtalent.com is one of the pioneering sites, in providing pre-employment net work. This has made the process faster and compressed.

Referring back with the previous employer about the candidature is also prevalent. So many candidates provide in their CV about their experience with big MNCS. How they worked and why they were sent out will be verified.

In Govt. Jobs, both State and Central Govt., a long drawn procedure of antecedents verification by intelligence bureau is a must. Unless the IB clears the name, appointment letters are not issued. The IB official personally verifies the details of the candidate at his place of residence for the last 5 years and certifies the merits of the candidate. Affiliations with political party, any pending police case are verified.

It is told that 30 years back one Gentleman got selection to IAS, but his antecedents were not cleared due to his participation in a political party meeting during his college days. He could not join. Later he started an IAS coaching center at Delhi and trained hundreds of successful.

6

101 Interview Questions

SECTION I

Puzzles

When faced with puzzles in interviews, don't be too much worried about giving the perfect AND correct answer. If you know the answer, you are safe, but if you don't know the answer, don't panic. Some of the puzzles may not even have a correct answer OR might have multiple correct answers OR the puzzle itself is based on a wrong premise. Puzzles are meant to evaluate how good the candidate is in applying his mind, making few assumptions and innovative approaches taken by him/her in solving the puzzle. Companies like Microsoft are known to use\puzzles to evaluate the candidates.

One practical advice with puzzles is to not jump to conclusion impulsively. Even if you have heard the puzzle before don't hesitate to get more details and ensure that the assumption and premise that you are making are the same that the interviewer also is making. In the software industry, employees are referred to as consultants. As consultants of software services you are supposed to ask as many questions as possible to gather all the requirements of the customer. That quality is also something that the interviewer is looking for in you.

During my Oracle days I attended a consultative skills training program. In the program, we were taught how to be good consultants. The trainer said, "When in front of a customer, ask as many questions as possible with the intent of gathering more information". Someone in the room asked "What if the customer is asking all the questions?", The trainer replied, "As a consultant, your answer should always be IT DEPENDS".

SOME PUZZLES

1. **Why do scooters and motor bikes have shock-absorbers and bicycles don't?**

   Ans: There can be multiple ways of answering this question. One is that shock absorbers for cycle are typically under the seat in the form of a metallic spring. Considering cycle's body weight is lesser than that of the motorbikes that provides enough cushion. Second is that cycle in countries like India is an economical mode of transport and hence cycle manufacturers have to be price conscious. Third answer could be that bicycles do have shock absorbers and are available in the market for a price. Some of the pricey ones even have gears in them.

2. **Why are most of the tractors of the world red in color?**

   Ans: There is no straight answer to this question. One way to answer could be that red is a primary color and also supposed to be the color of luck and hence is used more than other non-primary or metallic colors. Second way to answer could be that tractors are available now-a-days in all fancy colors as long as you are willing to pay the price.

3. **Why are most of the pencils hexagonal shaped and not any other shapes (triangle, square)?**

   Ans: One answer could be that you save wood by making them hexagonal. You can make 9 hexagonal pencils with the same wood that would be used to manufacture 8 cylindrical shaped pencils. Second answer could be that pencils that are hexagonal shaped don't roll off the table/desk or book where you keep them.

4. **If you are wearing a ring on your left ear and looking in a mirror in front of you and there is a mirror behind you, would the ring appear to your left or right in the 10th mirror image of yours?**

   Ans: This is a bit tricky question. You can imagine yourself as sitting in a barber shop to think through this. Barber shops typically have one large mirror in the front and another behind. Your image gets reversed but irrespective of whether it is the first reflection or 10th reflection it still appears reversed. Mirror image doesn't get reversed just because you are holding another mirror behind you. So, the left ear ring would become right ear ring.

5. **You have two hour glasses. One times 7 minutes and the other 11 minutes. Using these two hour glasses and nothing else, how would you accurately measure 15 minutes**
   Ans: This is a simple puzzle if you use both the hour glasses. You just need to take a moment and think through. Start both the hour glasses at the same time and after 7 minutes; flip over the 7 minute hour glass again. By the time 11 minute hour glass is finished, 7 minute hour glass would have taken 4 minutes. Flip over the 7 minute again and it will now take another 4 minutes. In all, 7+4+4=15 minutes

6. **Prove humans are more intelligent than computers?**
   Ans: You can start on a lighter vein on this question. If you were to ask a computer and request it to tell you whether to buy a clock that stopped working and shows 02:00PM or a clock that slows down 1 second every hour. Computer would suggest you to buy the clock that doesn't work because the clock at least shows correct time twice a day. Whereas clock that slows down 1 second would take few years to show correct time

7. **Design a remote control for the blind**
   Ans: The requirement is not complete and you should use the opportunity to ask the interviewer to provide more detail. What is the remote control intended for? Let us assume, the remote control is for music system. One way to answer could be by finding out if it is really mandatory to design a hand-held remote control. Why not choose the option of voice controls for the music system? A system that when powered can be operated using voice controls like play, rewind, forward, pause etc If the interviewer is not keen on building a voice control system and wants a hand held remote to be designed then you can think of the below (a) Remote that will allow him to detect the direction of the music system (b) Braille based buttons (c) Large size buttons than the normal size for ease of operation (d) Ease of navigation by providing identification keys

8. **Why the steering wheel of a car always is circular shaped whereas that of bikes is not?**

   Ans: While the steering wheel can be of any shape, any other shape like Triangle or rectangle would result in pointed edges and in an accident situation can prove fatal. Motor bikes have 2 wheels and cars have 4 wheels. This also means that the control is better with a wheel than a handle bar.

9. **At touchdown, are the tires of an airplane in motion or stationary?**

   Ans: They are stationary. If they are in motion there is a likelihood of plan catching fire due to friction and heat that would get generated in turn. If you observe closely, airplane tread pattern are smooth with not too many grooves like the regular automobile tires

10. **Why do most ads of watches show 10:12:40 as the time?**

    Ans: One answer is that it allows watch manufacturers to clearly display their company name and logo in between the hands. Second answer could be that the arrangement of the watch hands in this formation resembles a smile.

    If asked then why do digital clocks also show the same time, then the answer could be that the marketing and ad agencies are just carrying off the old legacy

11. **Consider a pendulum clock. What is the angle between the minute hand and hour hand when the time is 1515hrs**

    Ans: NOT ZERO The question could be meant to puzzle you. The answer definitely is not ZERO. If you think a pendulum clock doesn't necessarily mean analog clock. It could be digital display as well. So, the consideration and angle doesn't arise. Second answer could be arrived at by arguing that 12 hours make 360 degrees and at 1500hrs the clock hands would be at 90 degrees. After 15 mins, the minute hand is on 3 but the hour hand has moved away and hence the answer is not ZERO. It is 7.5 degrees

12. **A hunter walks 10 kms south and 10 kms east. He then kills a bear and drags it 10 kms north back to the base. What is the color of the bear?**

    Ans: White. The only place on earth where you could walk south, east and north and return to your base is north pole. Most certainly all polar bears are white in color. Hence, you can say with confidence that the color of the bear would be "white"

13. **There are 12 billiard balls of equal size, shape and color. One of them is either heavier or lighter than the others. Using not more than 3 weighing chances you should find the odd ball. Ans:** This is a tricky question because we are referring to 12 balls and not 8. We are also referring to not knowing whether the defective ball is lighter or heavier. Always use a pencil and paper approach for solving puzzles like this. Let us say you split the balls into 3 groups of 4 each and name them Grp 1, Grp 2 and Grp 3.
    1 Weigh Grp 1 and Grp 2
    (a) Weigh same – Discard the 8
    2. Weigh 3 known from Grp 1 or Grp 2 v/s 3 unknown from Grp 3
    (a) Weigh same – Then take the odd ball and weigh against any other to figure out if is lighter or heavier
    (b) Weigh different – Unknown group would also by now tell you if the odd ball is heavier or lighter
    (i) Take 2 balls out of the unknown group
    1. Weigh Same – Odd ball is the 3rd ball
    2. Weigh different – Identify odd ball from the two

14. **A snail is at the bottom of a well that is 20 feet deep. Every day it climbs 5 feet upwards and drops 4 feet in the night. How many days will it take for the snail to climb out of the well? Ans:** 16 days. There is a trap here. 20 is not the right answer. You might think "1 feet" is the difference every day and hence the answer. Always use paper and pencil. Day 1, it climbs 5 feet and in the night falls 4 feet. So, on Day 2, it is 1 feet above the well. Hence, on Day 16, the snail will climb out of the well.

15. **What common mathematical symbol when placed between 4 and 5 as shown below will result in a number that is greater than 4 but less than 6? 4 5**

    Ans: Mathematical symbols need not necessarily be operators. Put a decimal between the two and it becomes 4.5

SECTION III
Behavioural

Another popular form of interviewing is known **BEI** (Behavioral Event Interview). This is a new style of interviewing that more and more organizations are adopting. The premise on which this technique is based is that your past performance is a true indicator of your future performance in a similar situation.

STAR is one of techniques used in BEI. STAR stands for Situation, Task, Action and Results.

Situation – Describe the specific situation with the whole focus being on U.

Task – Describe the goal that was accomplished.

Action – Actions initiated by you that addressed the situation with appropriate amount of detail and again keeping the whole focus on U.

Result – Describe the results and the outcome of your actions. Don't shy away from taking credit yourself.

Situational questions require you to be as precise as possible and talk quantitative and provide supporting evidence if you can. Preparing for these questions require you to recall recent situations, make brief notes, create a story board around it and ensure the results reflect good on you. If possible, ensure you change the example based on the question and don't try to use the same example for all situational questions. It always helps to be honest.

16. Have there been any instances in the recent past when you realized the project failed because of your wrong decision?

Ans: There could be multiple reasons for asking this question. It could be to judge if you gracefully accept your own mistakes OR it could be to understand the lessons learnt. In either case, you should be prepared to share your experience.

How To :

I neither shy away from taking decisions nor shy away from taking blame. As far as I'm concerned, THE BUCK STOPS WITH ME. I was asked by customer to start a project in a week's time and since I didn't have resources on hand I decided to hire subcontractors. Subcontractors attended knowledge transfer sessions from customer and within 1 week of completion of knowledge transfer sessions in Switzerland quit and picked another offer from our competitor. It was a wrong decision and I learnt my lesson not to start a project with all subcontractors on a projects and plan for proper backups.

17. **You believe you have a better way of designing the solution but your team is not in agreement with your consideration, how would you convince them?**

Ans: There will always be different solutions to the same problem. In the rush of the hour it is very difficult to change the course of the project based on a suggestion. Especially when the other members disagree with you. One approach that would help in those cases is to build a small prototype and by not jeopardizing your current project schedule. Once you demonstrate you then have a better chance of your team listening to you. Let us say in spite of all this the team still doesn't merit your solution, then, you should move along with the team, support them and not try to jeopardize other's idea.

18. **What would you do if you are frustrated and unhappy with your project/manager?**

Ans: You should have an active discussion with your manager and provide your inputs at regular intervals. Most of the companies have 360 degree feedback in place. For some reason let us assume your organization has not implemented 360 degree feedback, you should then approach your manager first and if there is no reprieve approach your manager's manager either in the form of skip meetings or asking for a skip meeting.

* 360 degree feedback means that each employee is assessed by his subordinates, his manager, his peers and external/internal support organizations. Hence, you always have a way to express your unhappiness.

* Skip meeting is a meeting where you get to meet your manager's manager at a scheduled time

19. **What steps have you taken when attrition in your team has been 10% more than that of your company's average?**

Ans: Quoting real life examples would really help in answering this question. What we provide below is only suggestive in nature.

How To :

There was a rumor in the company that one of the product groups that I manage is being sold off. That spread like wild fire and I was losing team members on a regular basis. In this case the concern was due to the so called future uncertainty involved and job security. I organized a meeting and invited all the team members and the VP of my group to address them. I had clearly discussed the attrition issue with my VP and requested him to step in and help. My VP addressed the gathering and assured all employees that they would not lose their jobs and quelled all rumors about product sale. He talked about the product roadmap for future and assured job guarantee for all the employees who continue with us.

20. Instances in the last 6-12 months where your innovative solution has helped improve productivity

Ans: These needs to be given an individual touch and you cannot refer what we give here. What we have listed below is purely suggestive and sample in nature. So, think through and arrive at your own list.

How To:

1. I was part of a team that was designing a web store for a mobile manufacturing company. The website had to display category of products and upon selection of category has to display all products/ models and their images. Upon selection of a model, we need to display more details like specification, price and features. After all this, placing the order would take another 4 different screens. In all, the user would have to navigate some 8 screens and click 15 different places to place an order. I came up with a design where I reduced the screens to 3 and clicks to 3 by regrouping and providing the right filters. This was appreciated by my group manager and customer

21. Tell us an instance where you took a task that was outside your job description?

Ans: Use this opportunity to impress upon the interviewer that you go beyond your job definition. You can talk about company level initiatives that you have participated in. They could be corporate social responsibility (CSR) activities such as helping flood victims, teaching for orphanage kids over weekends etc. OR initiatives such as IP (Intellectual Property) awareness within the company.

22. **Tell us an instance where you took a decision without your manager's consent?**
Ans: Interviewer is trying to see if you can operate independently and take decisions on your own through this question. The way I would have answered this question is in the negative. You can say that you don't take your manager's consent for your day to day activities. I only "consult" my manager if the decision goes beyond my approval capacity and that involves larger scheme of things. You take your decisions and you are responsible for the decisions taken by you.

23. **Tell us an instance where you took a decision with limited known facts and the decision later proved to be right?**
Ans: If you are a lead or manager level employee then you would agree that decision making is complex and there will always be uncertainties involved. You can categorize decisions into routine day to day decisions (operational) and exceptional. Most of the routine day to day decisions are easy to make and you would have data and experience to take them. Exceptional cases require different handling and typically don't have much data on hand.

24. **What is your reaction, if told, the interview till now has been pathetic?**
Ans: There could be two reasons for saying something like that. One to see how you react even when you have been doing well in the interview and second reason is that you really didn't fare well. Let us say it is to test your reaction then you should gracefully accept his feedback and say that you have attempted all the questions to your best of ability and that may be there is mismatch in your profile and there requirement. If your interview really has not gone well, then you can thank him for having spent his valuable time with you and acknowledge that you didn't meet his expectation for whatever reason and assure him that given an opportunity you can always meet his expectation and perform to his satisfaction.

SECTION III
Case Study

Case study interviews are based on case description. Case study based and behavioral interviews have become more popular now-a-days. Case study based interview questions are used more prominently for consulting jobs and jobs that require analytical skills. Preparation for these interview questions is by far the most dreaded and most difficult. In the case of case study based interviews you would have to use your past experience, knowledge of the subject to analyze the case description.

25. We hire you to start a new practice around integration. How would you go about?

Ans: Before you attempt to answer the question, you should gather more detail from the interviewer

1. What are the business drivers for starting this new practice?
2. What is the plan/target for this financial year and next?
3. Does the company plan to groom internally or hire externally?
4. How well equipped is the sales team around integration?

The answers to the above questions allow you to frame your answer. For the sake of discussion we have presented the answers below in the same order

1. EAI and BPM are becoming hugely popular and companies are willing to invest and connect their systems
2. 100 member team by Dec this year
3. Hire and groom
4. We have hired a sales lead from WIPRO

How To:

Competency has 4 pillars namely and I would build competency activities around those

1. **Delivery**
   (a) Reuse artifacts
   (b) Productivity improvement tools
2. **Presales**
   (a) Build demos
   (b) Build Pilots
   (c) Build marketing material
3. **Enablement**
   (a) Conduct internal/external trainings
   (b) Encourage team to take external certifications

4. **Thought leadership**
   (a) Publish white papers
   (b) Participate in seminars/events

26. **You are working in a matrix organization and being a project manager of the same you realize none of the resources report to you directly but reported solid line into their respective departments and dotted line into you for the duration of the project. What style of management would you adopt in this organizational structure?**

    Ans: This is like "KING without a KINGDOM". You need to manage the show but the team doesn't report to you. It has its own set of challenges. Few things that you can adopt could be to agree upfront with the respective departments to ensure that his feedback is taken into consideration during the employee appraisal cycle and that communicated to the employees. You should also agree upon an escalation channel within the respective departments to ensure you have their support during the execution.

27. **A relative of yours is directly reporting to you. Would you postpone his or her promotion because your subordinates might feel you are favoring your relative?**

    Ans: Nepotism is a serious offense in the corporate world. HR has formulated strict policies around this. In large companies and MNCs you would rarely come across a situation like this. You should avoid hiding any such detail with your manager. If you have a relative of yours who has made to report to you, you should bring it up with your manager and HR upfront and ask him/her reporting to be changed to avoid any conflict of interest later. In the case where the manager and HR are fine with the relative reporting to you, then, you need not worry about delaying his/her promotion, as long as his performance deserves a promotion

28. **Your manager assigned a task to you over the weekend and mentioned she is travelling for the next 1 week on personal vacation and asked you to complete the task in her absence. She is not available over phone/email. What would you do? Ans:** Even if the manager was available on phone/email you should avoid disturbing him/her during their personal vacation unless there is an emergency situation

How To

As a responsible manager she would ensure all the required detail has been made available to me to operate in her absence. Since the task is critical and has to be accomplished during her absence I would also take down the name/contact of someone else who can coach/guide me during her absence.

29. Your team member is a Muslim and takes time off to offer Namaz during critical project schedule. How would you handle that situation?

Ans: This is a very sensitive topic and can also lead to employee filing a harassment suit if you interfere with his personal life. As long as someone is sticking to his project schedule and able to accomplish the tasks assigned to him/her, what he/she does beyond is their personal life. Even otherwise, as per company rules and business ethics, you cannot discriminate an employee in the name or religion, sex or caste.

* In middle east (Dubai, Saudi Arabia) and in other countries, designated areas have been created within offices to allow employees to offer their prayers.

30. We hire you as the head of Java practice and ask you to go and provide a compelling story to the prospects about our Java practice. How would you go about?

Ans: Instead of answering this question right away, you should seek a lot more information from the interviewer and then frame your response.

How To:

Seek answers to the below from the interviewer

1. How large is your java competency
2. What is the role wise split
3. What type of projects are being executed today
4. What is their bench strength
5. What type of intellectual property on Java do they have
6. What are their common customer complaints

SECTION IV : Traditional

Traditional interviews are by far straight forward questions based on your experience or resume. These are typically leading questions. You can easily make out what the interviewer is seeking from the question. It is always a good idea to have canned, readymade answers for these questions Companies have adopted other techniques in addition to traditional as it is easy to fool the interviewer in a traditional interview style. You will find these and hear these questions as they are commonly used in interviews and are easy to answer with little or no preparation.

32. Did you Find our Office Easily?

Ans: These questions are meant to be ice breakers and to make the interviewee/you more comfortable. Use the opportunity to open up and get comfortable. Always do your research in finding out the route and exact location of the office. You can use the opportunity to open up a discussion around an area of interest to you and modulate it to get comfortable with the interviewer.

How To:

Let us say you want him to focus on your experience with Infosys. You can start with something like this. "Thanks for asking. Yes, I was easily able to locate your office. I was working for Infosys as a delivery manager earlier and we had our corporate office in the same area. That is how I know this place".

Tip: Always reach the interview location at least 15 mins before schedule. If you are seriously looking out for the job and have not been to that company/location before, you can always travel to the interview location one day before to get comfortable with the route.

33. What do you know about Our Company?

Ans: This gives you an opportunity to show that you have done your ground work. Check out the company's website and learn more about the company and pick interesting tit-bits from here and there. For instance, if you find from the website that the company has been awarded best employer in India, make a mention about that. You can also ask the interviewer to explain more about their company.

34. Why are you Leaving your Current Job?

Ans: Always keep one or two good reasons handy. Be honest and reasonable in your response. Avoid bad mouthing your previous company or previous boss/manager. Try to bring out the attempts you have made to correct the situation and why you finally decided to leave. You should not make it look a decision taken in haste.

How To:

"Looking for an onsite opportunity and the company didn't provide which led to the decision to quit. I requested the company 1 year back to provide an onsite opportunity as I felt that would allow me to improve customer facing skills. Company did promise me but has been unable to provide me the opportunity. Discussed this with my manager multiple times but unfortunately the project within our group didn't have much onsite work"

35. You have changed jobs frequently (almost every 2 years). Why should we believe that you will stay with us longer?

Ans: IT industry has a bad reputation and employees frequently shift jobs. Employee stickiness you see in other industries is typically 4-5 times more than IT industry. If employee loyalty in non-IT sector is 12-15 years average then it is 3-4 years in IT sector. You should always reason out why you had to switch companies and give confidence that.

36. What are your strengths?

Ans: This should be well rehearsed and prepared. Don't try to create an answer during the discussion or start the conversation by saying… "Let me think…"

How To:

My strength lies in my ability to work as a team. I get along with team members easily and don't hesitate to seek help or provide help. I have also been awarded the best team player award twice in my career.

37. Why do you think you deserve being considered for this position?

Ans: This question could be asked in the beginning of the interview or towards the end.

Beginning of the interview

I believe in the saying "attitude decides your altitude". I have the right attitude to learn, adopt and perform. These core values have helped in succeed in all my previous organizations. In addition to that my experience meets the job description. Hence, I believe I deserve the job.

End of the interview

Selection of a candidate is decided on his experience and performance in this interview. My experience meets the requirement you have and my performance in the interview as per my assessment has been good.

38. What are the qualities in you that are criticized most by your managers?

Ans: In this question the interviewer is not just trying to get your weakness but also looking for validation, in the form of criticism by your manager. You can play smart and use the criticism to your advantage. You should always perform a SWOT (Strengths, Weaknesses, Opportunities and Threats) analysis on yourself. Keep one or two weaknesses and what you are doing to improvise ready.

How To:

Let us say you are poor at time management, talk about how you used to miss schedules earlier and what you have been doing proactively in the last 6-12 months to improvise.

39. If you were to make a career beginning again what would you change?

Ans: This question can be answered in many ways. These questions are meant to open you up and make you comfortable.

How To:

I would like to become an entrepreneur and start a company and put all my heart and energy behind it. The market has huge potential and there is no dearth of ideas. I would want to create job opportunities for others.

40. Industry is going through recession and cannot afford to pay you the salary you are currently drawing or last drawn. What percentage lesser salary would you be willing to join us?

Ans: This is a difficult question and the answer would vary depending on your situation, background and need.

Out of Job

If you are out of job and market is going through a recession period OR you have been given 3 month period by the current employer to find a new job, then, you might want to get into negotiations and arrive at a salary that meets your immediate needs.

Interest area

If the job is in your interest area OR job is something that you have been eagerly waiting to get into, then, you should be willing to sacrifice a portion of your current salary. You can always expect to get back to your salary or better salary once the market picks up again.

Comfortably placed : If you are doing very well in your current job and just exploring other options, then, you need not take the adverse step of taking a cut. You can always wait and explore more options.

41. Where do you see the software industry 5 years from now?

Ans: You can start this on a lighter note by saying I don't want to make the same mistake Bill Gates made few years back by trying to predict what software industry would be like in 10 years from now. He then had to correct himself. According to me, Change is fast and constant in the software industry. If anything, in 5 years from now, the industry will see more and more adoption of computers and penetration across the globe.

42. Where do you see yourself 5 years from now?

Ans: You need to give a personal touch to this question. We have provided suggestive answers below

How To :

1. Flying a private jet, owning a palatial bungalow and running a company of the size of Infosys
2. Vice President in your company
3. Speaker at the "Global Tech Days" seminar

43. Which one do you rate higher? Compensation or work environment?

Ans: The answer depends on the stage of your career and personal needs. In spite of that both are important for each individual. For each individual after he/she reaches certain compensation level would like to get more recognition and status in the form of work environment that is created around him/her. Hence, both are important but after a certain stage one takes precedence over the other.

44. How important is physical fitness for you?

Ans: In the computer industry due to lack of any form of physical exercise and high mental strain they are prone to health disorders like diabetes, BP and heart attacks. Hence, physical fitness is an important thing. Most companies today provide a gym, swimming pool and other games as options. You can talk about your fitness regime like going to the gym, your favorite sport etc.

45. What was the last training you attended in the last 6 months?

Ans: Keep this data handy before you attend the interview. Sample provided below

1. Intellectual Property 2. SOA design principles.

46. 3 Things you remember the most from the training you attended recently?

Ans: Keep this data handy before you attend the interview. Sample provided below

How To:

I attended a training program on Intellectual Property protection recently. The 3 things I remember are

1. Intellectual capital when legally protected becomes IP
2. IP is 3 forms

   (a) Copyright (b) Trademark (c) Patent
3. Global patent application form is called PTC.

47. We would like to contact your current employer to verify the details before we offer the job to you? Are you fine?

Ans: This question is similar to Q No: 68. Refer to the answer provided there. In addition to that, make sure they don't get in touch with your current employer before they officially release the offer to you and you accept the offer.

48. What is your notice period?

Ans: Notice period is the time you take to join the new company. The period between your resignation and last day in the current company. This is mentioned clearly in all the employment offer letters OR listed in the company policies. Some companies allow buying the notice period. Which means you can pay the notice period salary and leave them immediately.

49. What is your salary expectation?

Ans: Quote your current salary, provide a break-up of the same and then talk about your expectation. Always keep some scope for negotiation. If you are expecting a salary hike in your current company in a month or two, then include an average hike % to your current salary for your calculation purpose.

50. Are you willing to relocate?

Ans: You can be candid as far as this question is concerned. You can also seek more information from the interviewer on what he means by relocate. You can also find out the type of relocation package they have. You can also specify your preference and the reasons if you have a choice.

51. How much travel in a quarter would you be open to?

Ans: You can state any travel limitations you might have. Unless otherwise stated companies would expect you to take up travel and assignments in different parts of the country/world. Some jobs might warrant travel every month or quarter. Based on your job description you need to be prepared to address this. Also, seek information from the interviewer on what their requirement is and what type of travel policy they have (if the travel is going to be very frequent).

52. You took 2 years break in between your studies/employment. What were the reasons?

Ans: Talk through the reasons and explain when that took place and how you utilized that time. It will help to focus on what learnings have emerged by taking that break. For instance, if you took a 2 year break to take up higher studies mention that and how that significantly helped in your job.

53. What can you do that someone else cannot do?

Ans: You could start by saying that to answer this question honestly is something that you can do that others cannot. This is a question that needs to bring out your strengths. Analyse them carefully and have to be in line with what you have documented in your resume.

54. What awards/recognition have you received in your professional career?

Ans: Have all your award/certifications available for reference and show case them

1. Team awards
2. External awards
3. Individual awards
4. Service awards
5. Spot awards
6. Annual awards
7. Certifications.

55. Do you have any thing more to say?

Ans: Use the opportunity to seek more information/clarifications. Find out the next steps after this interview. Find out how long would the whole process take. Never ask the interviewer an immediate feedback on your interview. There are two reasons for that. One is that interview typically is done by 2 or more people and hence they would want to regroup and judge you. Second reason is that you have not allowed the interviewer to peacefully think through and analyze you.

56. What is the maximum team size you have handled?

Ans: I have seen many interviewees falter on this question. Either they give a number that is different from what is mentioned in the resume OR they give a number and when you ask them for a split of the team, it doesn't add up. In all, this question also is meant to judge your honesty and integrity. Never try to fool around and quote a big number to show that you have the right experience and exposure. Always do your preparation properly.

How To:

I have managed a team of 20 members. 5 of them were onsite and the rest were at offshore. At offshore, I was supported by 2 leads and 1 lead at onsite. One of the two offshore leads was a QA lead and the other development lead. So, in short, my direct reports were 3 and indirect 20.

57. Describe your organization structure?

Ans: Each organization has a different structure and different meaning to a similar title. For instance, a senior manager in some companies is a level below Vice President/Partner, whereas, it is not in the others. Always define your title, your role and what level you are in the organization ladder.

How To:

I'm a senior developer and report to a team lead. As a senior developer, I'm responsible for code development and design discussions. A senior developer is level 3 in the organization. We have 10 levels in the organization. With Level 1 being Associate/ Trainee and Level 10 being Executive Vice President

58. Have you terminated any employee in your career?

Ans: This is an interesting question and posed to test your mettle. Every team, group, division or company have bottom 5. Bottom 5, by definition, are people who are non-performers. While answering this question you need to present a wholesome case to show how you went about taking the decision and implemented it.

How To:

Our company has a process in place to recognize the Bottom 5% ever year. The exercise starts with appraisal cycle. After all employees have been appraised, we rank them relatively into 3 groups. Top 25%, Middle 70% & Bottom 5%. Once the bottom 5 have been identified, we inform them as to why they have been ranked in Bottom 5% and then put them on a PIP (Performance Improvement Plan). PIP is monitored directly by HR and the individual's performance measured for 3 months. If the performance doesn't improve then the employee is asked to leave. It is part of our company culture to promote performance.

59. As per company policy, employees can only travel to US on H1/L1 visa. Most of your team members for whom you processed H1/L1 Visas traveled happily the first time but then give some reason or the other to escape/avoid travel. How would you handle the situation?

Ans: One way to answer the question could be as described below:

How To:

Almost all companies across the industry who do business in the USA today have this issue. More so for companies that have majority of their business coming from USA. I don't know if there is any answer to this problem but we have tried to address this internally in our group by putting a refusal system in place. We record the refusal of employee carrying a valid visa and permit them to do so on 3 occasions. Anything beyond that gets escalated to the group head of our division and that could result in a penal action.

60. Describe your daily schedule?

Ans: On a lighter note, I heard a candidate say "2 punches and 1 lunch". Obviously, the interviewer is not interested in knowing your tea and lunch break details.

* Punch - Employees are required to swipe in and swipe out when they enter and leave the campus/office. This gets recorded as their in time and out time

How To:

We have given 2 sample descriptions. One for a developer level resource and the other for a manager level resource.

Developer

I work in a project that follows SCRUM methodology. We all assembly at 10:00 in the morning and have a quick 30 minute meeting to discuss the status and what work is pending. I then discuss design considerations with my team members and also work with the QA team for my component. Before leaving for the day, I post the progress made, what is pending and challenges being faced by me.

Manager

I manage a 30 member project team. I spend 20% of my time attending meetings with customers or my team or communicating. I spend 50% of my time coordinating the activities, monitoring and recording the progress. I spend 20% of my time issue resolution and tracking issues/risks and the rest conducting interviews, trainings or any other corporate responsibility activity.

61. How well do you work under stress?

Ans: You can be honest about your ability to take risk. Quoting a recent experience of yours would always help. You can talk about what actions have you taken to reduce the stress for yourself and for the team.

62. **Is your BOSS always correct?**

Ans: This is an old saying and doesn't hold true in most of the large software companies. In software companies and MNCs you are trained to express your opinion and **not always be the "YES SIR" type.** At GE, as part of their induction into the company, they are asked to debate on the two statements below

1. **Jack Welch is one of the best CEOs of the century**
2. **Jack Welch is an Ass Hole**

The debate is intended to encourage open discussion and participative culture · Jack Welch was the CEO of GE and one of the most successful CEOs of the century.

63. **What do you hate about your boss?**

Ans: You can answer it based on your experience. You should avoid bad mouthing your previous manager/boss or company. Try to subtly put across your point

How To :

He is poor at time management. He is always late for meetings. The common joke is that when he says he will be back in 2 minutes, it is typically 2 hours.

64. **What do you like about your boss?**

Ans: You can answer it based on your experience.

How To :

He is an excellent people manager. He always encourages all the team members. He gets involved in the discussions and also helps people build their careers.

65. **Are you good at managing time?**

Ans: We offer a unique way of answering this question. You can start off on a lighter note like we describe below

How To:

No one knows exactly when time started and when the time ends. This means, if you were to draw a time line, then, we don't know the start and end? This makes it an infinite line. Hence, you are always on-time.

66. **Are you a risk averse person?**

Ans: You can answer this question based on your nature. We have covered both type of profiles below

Risk Averse

My risk taking ability is dependent on the company's risk taking ability to some extent. I work for a very conservative company and it is more to do with company culture. Having said that, I can always mould myself.

Risk Taker

I take calculated risks. That too after doing all the required ground work. For instance, our company was exploring ideas on growing our business in the new financial year. My suggestion was to expand our base in the emerging markets like Middle East and China. I presented some data on the market opportunities, investment required, challenges and how we can overcome them.

67. In spite of India being a major power in the IT industry, why is that we still don't see too many MADE IN INDIA software products?

Ans: This is an interesting question and we provide some help below in answering this question.

How To :

India is considered a leader in the software industry but majority of the work we do is in the services business (application development, customizations, support, testing and BPO). Product development requires considerable amount of investment and venture funding. We in India have lacked that for some time and hence US has a huge lead over India. That trend has been changing in the last 5 years and we now have Indian companies seeking venture funding and starting new products from India.

68. After making an offer, as part of background verification, if we were to speak to your BOSS, how would he describe you?

Ans: It always a good idea not to burn bridges when you change companies. Most of the companies look for references and hence having your ex-manager reference-able always helps.

How To:

I still maintain a very good relationship with all my managers and ex-managers. You can also look at my LinkedIN profile which has recommendations from all my ex-managers and current manager.

69. After making an offer, as part of background verification, if we were to speak to your subordinates, how would he describe you?

Ans: You can draw from our suggestion below

How To :

I have good professional relationship with my subordinates. A lot of them would also like to work with me in my company as well. That is a good validation of the fact that they like me. Having said that, I wouldn't like to "rock the boat" You can also look at my LinkedIN profile which has recommendations from my team members.

70. How do you manage underperforming resources?

Ans: This is similar to the question that we answered around termination. Refer to Q No. 58.

71. How do you derive the critical path of a project?

Ans: Critical path simply put it defines the length of the project. Each task on the critical path hence becomes critical task. Any delay to the critical path task would result in overall delay. So, by closely tracking the critical path tasks you can avoid any delays and ensuring you finish the project on time.

72. What is the difference between FP, T&M and T&M with CAP?

Ans: FP – Fixed Price – Preferred model if there are not many unknowns. Project is executed at a fixed price for the customer. Customer is happy with this model because he is immune to any increases in cost. T&M – Time and Material – Model is used when the technology is new or project requirements are not very clear and still evolving. Customer pays for the time spent by resources on the projects. T&M with CAP – Time and Material but with a maximum limit on revenue and expenses. Due to the unknown nature of requirements, there is always a possibility that these projects can get dragged forever. Hence, at times, customers put a limit on the cost by capping (CAP) it.

73. How do you calculate the project margin for your project?

Ans: Project margin is calculated by arriving at the revenue and costs. Revenue in the case of FP is what has been agreed with the customer and in the case of T&M is hourly or daily rate multiplied by the duration of the project. Cost includes the resource cost, overhead cost and other miscellaneous. Project margin is then calculated by deducting cost from revenue.

74. Do you prefer SCRUM (Agile) project management methodology over waterfall?

Ans: It depends on the type of project. If the project involves new technology or product development, then, you can prefer SCRUM methodology over waterfall. SCRUM allows you to demonstrate and take feedback from customer at regular intervals. It also depends on the customer and what his preference is. In most of the cases, customer would like your process to map into their process.

75. What is the difference between iterative model and agile model?

Ans: Agile also to some extent is iterative in nature but the big difference between the two lies around process and the execution model. Agile believes in making the process light weight and keeping documentation to a minimum. Traditional iterative model uses a project manager to coordinate and control the project whereas agile (SCRUM) believes in individuals being responsible enough to manage their own tasks. Every team member is either a PIG or CHICKEN in SCRUM. PIGs are performers or the core team members. CHICKEN is someone who gains by the work delivered by PIGs.

76. What has your experience been working in a GDM (Global Delivery Model) – Team members located across the globe?

Ans: If your company has global presence then you would for sure have experience working in GDM model. You should talk about one project/program that was executed in the GDM model.

How To:

I was asked to manage the ERP upgrade project for a bank in China. The project required 100 resources as the upgrade had to be done on multiple instances across the globe. Our team was split across our delivery centers in Pune, Gurgoan, Hyderabad and China. Pune and Hyderabad had large teams (40 each) and the rest in Gurgoan (15) and China (5). Hyderabad and Pune had project managers and Gurgoan and China had leads. I was the program manager working with all these groups remotely.

77. How do you manage resources in a GDM (Global Delivery Model)?

Ans: Refer to Q 77. In addition to that, having conference calls with all the team members and video/web conferencing at periodic helps. Maintain the project files in a central location accessible to all so that the progress can be tracked easily. Review of deliverables also helps tracking the progress.

78. How do you calculate attrition percentage of your team?

Ans: One way of calculating attrition is using the LTM model. LTM stands for Last Twelve Months. That means you take the headcount at the beginning of the year and the headcount at the end of year. Then removing any new additions that year and resignations of employees who joined and left within the 12 months. You are left with the headcount at the end of the year. The difference between the headcounts is your attrition rate.

79. What is the average industry attrition rate?

Ans: The attrition rate in the IT industry keeps varying but typically is between 14-18%. The number varies from product companies to services companies to BPOs. BPOs have higher attrition rates and are in the 30% and above range. Companies like Infosys, even though are not pay masters, boast of lower attrition rates of 10-12%. They achieve this through their brand image, good campus facilities and excellent employee oriented policies.

80. "Work from home" is a policy in your company. How would you manage a project in that environment?

Ans: Work from home requires that resources can work independently. Technologies that go hand in hand in the case of work from home include telephone connectivity, broadband internet and connectivity to office network. Employees should have good corporate internet connectivity. In addition, "hot seats" to be provided at office to allow employees to visit once in a while to download large files or connect with others. Use of web conferencing facility helps the team connect online and collaborative technologies like Confluence, Web Center help teams to work as a team on the same deliverable. Web 2.0 technologies like Wiki, Blog, Chat also help in making this work.

* "Work from home" policy allows employees to discharge their official work from home. Companies are shifting to this model as infrastructure costs are raising and the commutation time to office also is increasing.

SECTION V
Technical

Technical interview depends on the type of job and area of specialization. This section is aimed at IT professionals. This section is only a small sample of what can get asked.

Preparing for technical interview questions is very important. As we all know, IT technology is changing fast. What was relevant two years back is not relevant now and hence it is recommended that you always keep yourself abreast of the advances. Most of the IT companies today are seeking candidates with good technical knowledge. Even manager positions require technical depth. Survival of pure play managers in the IT industry is becoming difficult.

81. Describe SCRUM in 3 words?

Ans: SCRUM is Short, Iterative and Common Sense. SCRUM is an Agile methodology that is gaining a lot of Short - Project sprints are of 30-45 days. So, every 30-45 days you have a deliverable that can be shared with the customer for feedback

Iterative – You repeat the 30-45 day sprints till you accomplish all the requirements

Common Sense – Agile methodology relies a lot of common sense and removes all process related overhead

* This is author's definition. You can define it your own way.

82. Tell us about your experience in writing a program/algorithm/ design that was better than what the team proposed?

Ans: What we provide below is only suggestive. You should think through and use your own experience.

How To:

Company was planning to build a product and we had to embed a database to store data. Team had proposed options like storing it using a commercial light weight database. The problem with that approach is that you end up adding to the product cost. I explored the option of using open source and that integrated well into the product at no additional cost.

83. Company has requested you to build software that tracks the movement of laptops in and out of the company. What technology would you consider?

Ans: You should consider RFID based sensors and tags. RFID stands for Radio Frequency Identification. On the hardware front, we can put RFID tags on all laptops and RFID scanners can be installed at all entry and exit points of the building. RFID scanners can then scan the movement of assets like laptops. On the software front, Microsoft has BizTalk platform that has RFID platform that integrates well with the above said hardware.

84. Is Web 2.0 hype?

Ans: The answer is NO because 2.0 is signifying the advancement of web pages from static content to more interactive and collaborative. Wikis, blogs, video sharing sites are all examples of Web 2.0. Web sites that were otherwise considered autocratic have now become democratic by allowing users to post their opinions and share their thoughts.

85. What is Enterprise 2.0?

Ans: Social software used in enterprise context is referred to as Enterprise 2.0. It also means use of collaborative tools within the enterprise.

86. What design considerations would you assume when using AJAX

Ans: AJAX stands for Asynchronous Java Script with XML. Design considerations like browser support, Java Script activation in the browser and development time should be kept in mind.

87. What are the disadvantages of using AJAX?

Ans: Use of history and back button has some challenges and design should keep those considerations in mind. Sequence of the fields on the screen also should be kept in mind when using AJAX as it is asynchronous in nature.

88. What is the difference between DTD and XSD?

Ans: DTD stands for Document Type Definition and XSD stands for XML Schema Definition. DTD is an old specification for XML definition. It has been replaced by XSD. XSD has support for data types and you can precisely define the number of occurrences of each element

89. How do you SOA (Service Oriented Architecture) enable an organization?

Ans: Almost all organizations today are embracing SOA. SOA is a paradigm shift for organizations and hence they can adopt in stages rather than take a big bang approach.

- SOA requires strategic approach for maximum reuse and flexibility
- SOA need not mean the same thing for everyone
- We should develop both process and people centric services SOA is not just about XML and ESB
- ROI takes longer

90. What are the different SOA maturity levels?

Ans: There can be different versions but most of them capture the same classification

Level 1

- Legacy integration
- Service based integration
- Information integration
- Self service

Level 2

- Legacy modernization
- Structured data movement
- Standardized collaboration
- Enterprise architecture
- Transformation

Level 3

- Infrastructure virtualization
- Composite applications
- Predictive business processes
- Software as Service

91. When asked to create a SaaS (Software as a Service) offering, what challenges do you foresee?

Ans: SaaS should keep the below in mind

(a) Multi-Tenancy

(a) How to support hundreds of organizations

(b) Security

(a) To ensure on company data is not being shared with the other

(c) Availability

(a) Requirements vary but one very important criteria

92. Name two design patterns you have used in your projects?

Ans: 1. Singleton – Restriction of instantiation of a class to one object. This is useful when only one object should exist in the system for that class

2. Façade – Hides the complexity and provides an easy interface to the outside world

93. What is ACID?

Ans: A – Atomic – Either all or none

C – Consistent – Commit or rollback to old consistent state

I – Isolation – Changes are only visible after committed

D – Durable – Changes are saved and not lost

94. What is the 1st Normal form?

Ans: One of the normal forms defined by E. Codd. A database table is considered to be in 1st Normal form, if the relation is free of repeating groups. For instance, lack of a unique key in a table violates FNF

95. What is MOM?

Ans: MOM stands for Message Oriented Middleware. MOM helps integrate disparate systems in the enterprise. It helps in sending and receiving messages across systems within and outside the enterprise. They also support routing and transformation of data.

96. What is DAD?

Ans: DAD stands for Distributed Application Development. It depends on multi-tier development architecture. A distributed application is like a client/server protocol in which you use a set of rules that specify a behavior for two collaborating processes. In a client/server relationship, one process (the client) initiates the interaction by issuing a request to a second process (the server). The server process must await a request from the client and, on receipt of that request, performs a service and returns a response (or result) to the client. The server is capable of handling requests from multiple clients and is responsible for coordinating and synchronizing responses

97. What is the difference between an abstract class and interface?

Ans: Interface has no implementation and only contains the definition. On the contrary, Abstract class can contain default implementation. Abstract class can also contain abstract methods and non-abstract methods. When you inherit from abstract class, the derived class should implement all the abstract methods

98. What is the common algorithm used in a recursive procedure?

Ans: A recursive algorithm is a method or set of steps that use a recursive definition of a problem to solve it. Such examples of recursive algorithms are palindrome, sorting, Fibonacci & factorial.

Factorial Algorithm fact(non-negative integer n)

```
{
  if(n==0)
      {
            return 1;
      }
            else
      {
            return fact(n-1)*n;
      }
}
```

The first if statement is called to find "Zero factorial". We return 1 in the case of n being ZERO. However, if it is called to find n!, it calls fact(n-1) (factorial of a slightly smaller number) and multiplies that value (once it is returned) by n, and returns that value.

99. What are the different architecture views according to UML?

Ans: They are Logical – End user perspective of the requirement – Sequence diagram and Use case are used to represent this Development – Programmer's perspective of the requirement – Component, Class and Package diagram are used to represent this Process – This deals with the dynamic aspects of the requirement. The interactions and the behavior. Activity diagram illustrates this Physical – System engineer's view of the requirement – Deployment diagram depicts this

100. What is the difference between static and dynamic diagrams in UML?

Ans: Static diagrams like Class diagrams show how the things are, their attributes and relation between different classes. Dynamic diagrams like sequence, activity show the action and interaction between the objects. For instance, one object calling another object

101. What is a primary use case and what are alternatives?

Ans: Primary use case is one that is the default flow in any use case. Alternatives are the exception flows.

ANNEXURE 1
INTERVIEWS : SUCCESS STORIES

Civil Services Results of 2009

Candidates applied for civils	:	4,09,110
Candidates appeared for prelims	:	1,93,091
Qualified for mains	:	12,026
Candidates invited for personal interviews	:	2,432
Successful candidates	:	875
		(Male 680 + Female 195 = 875)
General Category	:	399
OBC	:	273
SC	:	127
ST	:	76
Total	:	875

Over view :

Among the first 25 rankers 10 are female. Among the winners 44 are physically handicapped. 5 are visually handicapped. 11 has hearing problem. The cadre wise selection for 2010 is as follows.

Cadre	*General*	*OBC*	*SC*	*ST*	*Total*
IAS	66	38	18	9	131
IFS	15	10	1	4	30
IPS	77	39	21	13	150
Central Group A	298	159	81	44	582
Group B	57	27	06	06	96
				Total	875

Commission is maintaining a consolidated reserve list of 228 candidates – (General 114, OBC 88, SC 18 and ST 08).

Topper for year 2009 : Dr. Shah Faezal from Jammu and Kasmir.

Mr. Prakash Purohit – 2nd Rank – B.Tech from IIT Delhi.

Ms. Iva Sahay-3rd Rank - Graduate from JNU, Delhi (topper in Women)

Ms. T. Anupama – 4th Rank

Top 25 candidates comprise 15 males and 10 females.

Candidates selected from AP = 50

IAS topper 2009

Excerpts from the interview with Mr. Shah Faesal appeared in Civil Services Chronicle June 2010 issue is quoted.

IAS Topper : 2009

Shah Faesal, a Doctor from Kupwara district in Jammu & Kashmir has topped the IAS 2009 exams. Faesal made it in his first attempt. He completed his secondary School up to Class X in Kashmir Valley and MBBS from Sher-i-Kashmir Medical College, Srinagar. He choose public administration for Prelims and public administration and Urdu literature for Mains. His father Ghulam Rasool Shah, a School Teacher was gunned down 8 years back by militants. His mother Mebeena Begum motivated him for his preparation for Civils. He took coaching for Civils from Hamdard study circle at New Delhi.

Dedication, seriousness and madness to get into I.A.S. are the basic mantras for his success. Internet use was key for his preparation. He is a regular reader of Hindu, Daily. His preparation started in March 2009. After prelims, he started preparing for mains. He attended two mock interviews at Hamdard study circle before the personal interview.

Mr. Purusotham Agarwal was the Board Chairman for him in personal interview. Faesal is an MBBS graduate. So the initial questions in the interview were on health care. In General knowledge they asked him about China, Kashmir issue, Article 370 etc. The next question was on right to information Act, since he mentioned it as his hobby. He elaborated RTI as a tool for good governance.

Mr. Faesal says in an interview to 'Civil Service Chronicle' in June 2010 that **"Hard work, focused preparation, good reading material, thorough reading etc. are the prerequisites to crack the examinations. One should understand that this exam needs some extra mental make up".**

Mr. Faesal was congratulated by Dr. Manmohan Singh, Prime Minister of India when he met him in Delhi, since it is for the first time that a Kasmiri is topping in Civils. Faesal started preparation since Dec. 2008, but serious preparation started after medical internship in March 2009. He studied the book by Mr. Laxmi Kant on Public Administration and kept pace with current affairs. He is a regular contributor to Greater Kashmir Journal on current affairs.

He depended mostly on internet - wikipedia, Yahoo answers etc. He has chosen the topic Globalism Vs Nationalism for essay. Conceptual clarity is most important – says Mr. Faesal. **"Develop Good writing style, while attempting the answers. Better to answer 100% sure answers first. Then 70% sure answers. Negative marking stops the candidate from guessing".**

Madness to get into the IAS is the Mantra of his success.

Civils toper 2006 : Mr. Mutyala Raju

It is not an easy time to top the civil examinations. We can go through the achievements of Mr. Mutyala Raju topper in 2006 from Andhra Pradesh and learn how to prepare for civils. He hails from a very poor family and it has taught him to secure top ranks from tenth class onwards. He did his M.E. from prestigious Indian Insititute of sciences, Bangalore. He had coaching from Srirams, IAS, New Delhi. It became a habit for him to study well and get ranks in what ever examination he appears. He studied in Telugu Medium up to 10th class later when he joined polytechnic college at Tanuku, the English Medium created few problems. He learnt to write answers in English after reading the chapters. He never looked back. In the civils personal interview also he did it in English successfully.

When he was in II yr B.Tech the idea of attempting civils came into his mind. He does not know how to prepare. He does not know how many questions he has to answer in the General Studies paper. He studied for 2 months only. He got into the interview but did not succeed. He was less by 16 marks to get a rank. Second attempt pushed him to 223 Rank.

His only aim is to get IAS. He had a detailed plan. Along with two of his friends he hired a house and started studying individually. He observed candidates undergoing coaching at R.C. Reddy Institute and Brain tree. The inspiration is through different slogans they have around them in the hired room. He is left with 5 more months. He has completed the syllabus in half the time (2½ months). Daily he studied for 15 hrs. The timetable for preparation is as follows.

6.00 to 7 a.m. – reading daily News paper
8.30 to 12.30 a.m. – General studies
1.30 to 3.30 pm Mathematics
3.30 to 5.00 pm rest
5 pm to 8 pm Mathematics
9 pm to 2 am Electrical Engineering

Then the remaining 2½ months he has written mock tests to rectify his mistakes. He completed the mock tests in 2 hrs through the time given is 3 Hrs. It clearly tells that none shall feel that IAS is a herculian task and difficult to achieve. With his rural background and Telugu Medium studies at secondary school level he secured top rank with dedication. One cannot be pessimistic. Try to rectify your mistakes. The advise Mr. Muthyala Raju has given in an interview in may 2007 for Enadu (Telugu Daily) is reproduced in English :

"Don'ts:

- With the main aim to get through civils do not neglect your health. I did it and repented. In the third attempt I avoided extra strain. Unless your mind is cool, you cannot complete the exams properly.
- In case you are undergoing coaching, do not take coaching for each subject at different institutions. You will be loosing time. Better to confine to one institute for all subjects. Do not depend solely on the study material supplied by the institute.
- Think well before you select your optionals. Do not change the optionals once decided. Incase you get less score in the first attempt if you study well you may get good score next time. If it is a new subject for second time it is difficult.
- Do not elect optional with the misconception that you will have god score in it. Select optionals in which you have aptitude. Better to select optionals in which duration between two exams is more.
- My optional is Engineering but I did not take Engineering. Syllabus is very heavy. Question paper is lengthy. You will lose time in turning the question paper pages.
- Do not stress on any one subject say General studies or optionals. Give equal importance to all subjects.
- Candidates with English Medium are advised to read 'Hindu'; Telugu candidate: 'Enadu' Telugu.
- Do not attempt the exams if you are not sure to win.
- You get good rank with 55% marks. Do not feel bad if you have not done well in one paper. Attempt well in other paper.

- Civils preparation is prolonged. Do not loose confidence. Do not waste time."

Mr. Muthayala Raju is next to Mr. D. Subba Rao, IAS Topper in 1971 from Andhra Pradesh. Shri D. Subba Rao worked as Secretary, Finance, Government of India and Presently Governor, Reserve Bank of India (2009 onwards). After a gap of 36 years Mr. Raju topped the list from AP. He achieved it by rectifying his mistakes in the first few attempts. The recent trend in civils is to analyse major events happened in the country. The candidates have to analyze it in the Indian context and its repercussions. Then comes the international scenario. The advise he gives to the candidates is reproduced in English :

"Do's

- Plan to have systematic preparation. Make division of subjects and study them accordingly.
- Make a habit to read for more hours.
- Read only standard books.
- Assess your progress by yourself and go ahead.
- Prepare your own notes after reading newspapers. Relationship between India and Foreign countries, International affairs, social problems, important MOUs, and their effect on the country are to be kept in mind.
- By reading current affairs books; the replies by all candidates are stereo typed and you may not score well.
- Revision of subject is important. In a week I studied for five days and kept two days for revision.
- During the interiem period between prelims and main concentrate on mains and optionals.
- Understand the question carefully when you are in the examination hall. Write correct answer. It is a waste of time to fill the answer sheets. You will not get a good score.
- In the general studies (main) attempt statistics first. Don't keep it for last minute.
- Answer two marks questions after an hour, and not in the beginning.
- You cannot predict personal interview. It may move round a particular topic or on different subjects. Be prepared to respond – on bio-data, current affairs, optionals, previous jobs etc.
- Don't be pessimistic if you fail. Attempt more vigoursly and "rededicate."

Muthyala Raju's Personal Interview

Every one is anxious to know about IAS personal interviews. There are several stories around the corner. How many stair cases you have climbed ? etc. are told as stories. But the recent trend in the interviews has changed. Excerpts from the personal interview of Sri Muthyala Raju – topper 2006 IAS is reproduced below. (Published in Enadu, Telugu Daily).

Raju : May I come in Sir?

Chairman : Yes, please.

Raju : Good morning, Sir. Good morning, Madam. Good morning, Sirs.

Chairman : You are Mr…

Raju : (Still in standing position). Mutyalaraju Revu Sir. (Chairman is writing something. Other members are keenly watching the candidate.)

Member 2 : Please take your seat.

Raju : Thank you, sir.

Chairman : Mr. Revu, You did B.Tech from REC Warangal, ME from IISc, Bangalore. But why did you do diploma?

Raju : Sir, After completion of my 10th class, based on my financial background, my father joined me in polytechnic. After completion of polytechnic, we do get jobs. Also, since I will get scholarship, the amount of money spent on me is less.

Chairman : That means you will get job after diploma.

Raju : Yes Sir, I got a private job. Company is Cain energy limited.

Chairman : Then, why did you join B.Tech?

Raju : Sir, After completion of my diploma, I wrote EMCET and I got state 1st rank. So I convinced my father that I will join REC which is a premier Engineering institute in our state.

* * * *

Member 2 : You are in IPS for 4 months. So I can ask some questions.

Raju : Yes, Sir,

Member 2 : Are you aware that the confession admitted to police is not allowed as witness. Why ?

Raju : Yes sir. Confession admitted to police is not allowed as witness. Since there is always a possibility of getting the confession in the way police like, law doesn't allow it.

Member 2 : What is Res gestae?

Raju : Sir, All the circumstances leading to the same transaction are allowable as evidence.

Member 2 : You are on the line. Could you explain more?

Raju : (after 2-3 seconds), If some people wanted to commit dacoit and in the process if they theft a vehicle, eventhough theft of vehicle is not connected with dacoity but it is admissible as it forms the circumstance leading to dacoity.

Member 2 : Could you tell me the section which deals with Res gestae?

Raju : Sorry sir, I could not remember the exact section.

* * * *

Chairman: Your hobbies are meditation, motivating others and Indian Mythology. Don't you think that all are inward looking?

Raju : Sir, Whenever possible I play cricket in addition to my hobbies, which is a team game.

* * * *

Member 2 : Tell me which countries will reach final in the present world cup?

Raju : Sir, I think Australia and Sri Lanka.

Member 2 : Already two countries reached semifinals i.e., Sri Lanka and Newzealand. What do you think about other two?

Raju : Sir, I beg to differ with you. Actually three countries i.e., Sri Lanka, New Zealand and Australia reached semifinals. 4th team depends on the outcome of the today's match between England and South Africa.

Member 2 : Do you know about fly ash?

Raju : Sir, Thermal power stations produce fly ash while generating electrical power.

Member 2 : Which state is using it more? Definitely it is not Haryana, My own state.

Raju : Sorry Sir, I don't know

* * * *

Member 3 : (X-A).(X-B) has highest X power of 2. Do you agree?

Raju : Yes, Sir.

Member 3 : (X-A) (X-B) (X-C) has highest X power....

Raju : 3, Sir.

Member 3 : Then, tell me. What is the answer for (X-A) (X-B).... (X-Z).

Raju : (after 3-4 seconds), It must be Zero. Sir, because of the presence of the term (X-X).

* * * *

Member 1 : Your hobbies are meditation, motivating others and Indian Mythology. What you do in motivation?

Raju : Madam, many of my classmates and Juniors came to me for clearing their doubts in subjects as I am the toper of my class. I usually listen to their problems regarding their understanding of concepts as many have problems either in one or many subjects. I tell them that every subject is easy if you know the concepts clear and we should like the subject what we are studying...

Madam : Do your response is same for all?

Raju : Madam, I usually spend more time with those who are very much lagging. I take classes to clear their doubts.

Madam : Then do you call it motivation or strategic learning?

Raju : Madam, strategic learning may be the correct term.

Madam : What is the difference between these two?

Raju : Madam, motivation is a general term which includes not only academic motivation but also others like psychological, etc., Madam, I don't know exactly the meaning of strategic learning.

Madam : Which books you read in Indian Mythology?

Raju : Madam, I read Ramayana and Mahabharata.

Madam : Since your hobbies are motivating others and Indian Mythology, tell me how Krishna motivated Arjuna?

Raju : Madam, When Arjuna refused to fight with friends, teachers, Krishna told him that it is the duty of the king to protect Dharma and fight wars for protecting it. We should not move away from our duty. Since soul is immortal and of which is born, death is certain, of which death happened, birth is certain. Hence you should not think that you are committing crime. Also he motivated him by saying that we should do work only. We should not think about the results of our actions. Otherwise, attachment to the results will occur which is a major reason for unhappiness.

Madam : Do you practice it?

Raju : Madam, It is very difficult to practice.

Madam : Why?

Raju : Madam, for example, if we are about to play a cricket match, we will think about the winning of the match which is actually the result of the playing that match.

* * * *

Chairman : Thank you.

Raju : Thank you, Sir. Thank you, Madam. Thank you, Sirs.

We can observe how supplementary emerged from main question. It is important to note that members objected to his side tracking. The candidates can disagree with the members. He agreed his ignorance. He showed his gratitude when a member corrected him.

Other Toppers

- Ms. Sandeep Kaur a Punjabi selected in 2009 is the daughter of a Chaprasi in Morinda Thasil Office of Punjab. She is one among the three children.

Mr. N. Balaram (834 rank). He strived hard to get his livelihood at an early age. His attempts to get a job failed and he became an auto driver. He belongs to Palamur of Mahaboobnagar District (A.P). Palamur is famous for migrant labour. His parents Hunya and Keshi depended on agriculture. Without major income of livelihood the family struggled. Balaram worked as daily labourer. He got married with Sarada at the age of 18 in 1988. By the time he was a failed intermediate candidate. From Sciences he has changed his group to CEC. In search of livelihood he has shifted his family to Hyderabad. He hired an auto rikshaw after his failure to get a job. He was auto driver upto 2005. During the period through distance education he graduated with EPP subjects and MA with PPM. By the time he is the father of three children. He did his M.Phil from Osmanaia Unversity. That time he decided to compete for civils. His wife encouraged him by working in a cloth merchant shop at Hyderabad. Balaram got training from AP study circle at Hyderabad. In 2008 he succeed in main exams and 2009 he got selected in civils with 834 rank. He got Indian Revenue Services. In 2009 he attended group-I, Group-II interviews of AP Public Service Commission. But, luck did not favour him. He did not relent in his efforts. This is the success story of an young man. At the age of 30 he succeeded in fulfilling his dreams.

Ms. Amrapali : When the results were announced the family did not believe that she got through the civils. They checked up the UPSC website thrice to confirm that she got 39th rank. Prof. K. Venkat Reddy, retired Professor in Economics from Andhra University is her father. He belongs to Agraharam of Prakasam Distrct in A.P. His two daughters were brought up to in a way achieve their goals.

Amrapali studied 10th class at Visakhapatnam – Satya Sai Mandir School. She did her B.Tech. from IIT Chennai and MBA from IIM Bangalore. Her younger sister Manasa got 237 rank in civil services and is working as assistant commissioner – IRS, Bangalore. Amrapali prepared for the exams with in 18 months. She was not tempted to join software companies though her colleagues are earning 25 lakhs per year. She has a goal. She had love for books. She aims at women's education and women's development.

The result of 2009 show the clear determination of the candidates who reached the pinnacle of success with tireless hard work and study.

Personal interview is the main stage in civils. Interviews are conducted for about three weeks in April. In the severe competition it is difficult to get a score for personal interview. To get a rank in interview it is luck plus hard work and relentless effort.

If we go through the opinions expressed by different successful candidates to media after the ranks are announced, we can analyze the style of personal interviews. Since the civil service is the top most interview a candidate appears, it is taken as a model to others. Slightly the level of interview may change for other jobs. Overall it is the same. Performance of the candidate is more important. Always the Board members will try to make the candidate feel good.

Some of the experiences will be guiding force to aspirants.

Dr. N. Bharat Gupta student of Kurnool Medical College postponed his completion of Medicine to Feburary 2010 with an aim to complete the mains. He prepared for civils and in the first attempt itself he stood at 17th rank (2010). Instead of completing his MBBS in May 2009, he completed it in February 2010. He appeared personal interview in April 2010. He belongs to Gooty of Anantapur District – AP. Throughout his educational career he scored 90%. His farther Mr. Ramesh Gupta is a Senior Sectional Railway Engineer. Mother is a house wife. His sister is doing dental course (BDS). He completed his 10th class at Kendriya Vidyalaya, Gooty with CBSE syllabus and got 93%. He stood first in AP Residential Junior College in Intermediate with 96% marks. He scored 265th rank in EMACET entrance examinations for MBBS. In the first attempt he got medical seat in Govt. Medical College, Kurnool.

He concentrated on civils right from III year MBBS. His friend Dr. Vamsi Krishna inspired him for civils. He started his preparation in a principled manner. His friend's advise was always there. He prepared for the exams independently and did not approach any coaching centre.

During his house surgeon, he worked in the Hospital for 8 hours. Remaining leisure time he utilized for preparation. He slept for few hours. He got extension to complete internship from college authorities. Mean while he completed civils main examination.

He was interviewed for 30 mts. by the board of Mr. Nirbhay Sarma in April 2010. It was an easy affair for him except a question on – 'Vulavacharu' a rural reciepe – rasam and its preparation which he did not answer with ease. They questioned him about the first aid given to a patient suffering with chest pain and admitted in the hospital. He answered it very well and the board was very happy. The subsequent questions are about – Indian economy, green revolution, contribution of Dr. M.S. Swaminathan, Panchayat Raj System, duties of a district collector and magistrate, European union, situation in Punjab and others. Dedication and support from friends is his main forte. "God helped me" said Dr. Bharat Gupta to media persons. Mr. Bharat Gupta in an interview with Eanadu Daily dated 16-5-2010 explained his efforts for success.

"The original idea to prepare for civils came when I was a student of intermediate (+2). Lecturers and friends encouraged me at that stage since I was a merit student. During my internship at Kurnool Medical College, I attended on different types of patients. Some of them are suicide cases. I was surprised at the way they tried to commit suicide for simple reasons. When I discussed the issue with the patients and relatives it is amazing to note that financial problems are the main reason. Among them ryots, poor people are involved in committing suicide. I was perturbed. Instead of serving on them as doctor, I thought of serving them better as an IAS officer. Then itself I was determined to compete.

I am not bothered about the rank but to achieve IAS. I continued my preparations for civils. My optionals are Public administration and Anthropology. To be a successful civil servant one has to know the administration. To know more about social needs and human relations I studied anthropology. Being a student of medicine I scored better.

I did not restrict my studies with few books. I collected lot of books. I studied for a minimum of 10 hours per day. I analysed every thing in the angle of civils. For general studies I studied History by Mr. Agnihotri, Geography by Mr. Kullar, Polity by Dr. D.D. Basu, Lakshmi Kanth, Current affairs from Vaziram Material and Public Administration by **Fadia and Fadia. I could not complete reading Indian year book published by publications division. I might have improved the score if I have completed reading it.**

My interview was satisfactory.

Question : Who is the labourer from Andhra Pradesh who became Chief Minister?

Ans : Mr. T. Anjaiah and I explained about his administrative capacities.

The answers on district information was more than satisfactory.

It is not compulsory to attend coaching. It may help to some extent. Hard work is more important. Nothing is impossible. It is a myth that success in the first attempt is not possible. With determined effort, hard work and preparation one can succeed in first attempt. I will strive hard to implement government schemes to the deserving people. My main aim will be to control misappropriation of Government funds. I shall create minimum facilities to poor and needy. Mr. Gupta is the topper from AP State in 2009.

Belgaum to Hyderabad

Ms. Bharati belongs to Karnataka State. After marriage she moved to Hyderabad. She got IPS in 2008. In 2009 she achieved 59th rank and secured IAS. Hailing from a middle class family near Belgaulm – her father runs a whole sale medical shop. She studied degree at Belgaulm. She was selected by Karnatak Public Service Commission as Tahsildar and worked for 3 years. She secured high rank in the 2nd attempt. She was undergoing training for IPS at Sardar Vallabai Patel Police Academy, Hyderabad when she got selection for IAS.

History and Public Administration are her optionals. Mr. K.K. Paul Board in UPSC interviewed her in April 2010. Interview revolved around several subjects like –

Naxalism, Greyhounds Vs Salvajudum, Social Justice propounded by Dr. Ambedkar, Revenue Administration in Karnataka etc. The main question she expected was why you are opting for IAS, when you are already selected for IPS. But she did not face the question. But they asked her about the first women IPS officer, Ms. Kiran Bedi. They were happy with the reply.

> Her advise to the aspirants is simple. "Try with a clear goal, success is yours. Make it a habit to read English dailies to have general awareness about current events. By the time you graduate, worldly knowledge is necessary. Then we will not be wasting any time in learning things. It is easy to succeed."

The objective in her case is clear. She started her career as Group II officer in Karnataka State. She knew the powers of district Collector. She competed at National Level. She was not satisfied with IPS and appeared for improvement. Her social background is of middle class family. The goal is clear and she achieved it. Parents are not in administration set up and the place she hails from is not a metro. So, youth should emulate her. They should not be under the impression that candidates from towns only will get into IAS and sons / daughters of highly influential officer only get selected.

Son of an Agriculture Labour

Mr. Ch. Vijaya Rao competed in civils leaving M.Phil study at Central University of Hyderabad in 2009. He lost his mother at a very young age. Father was an agriculture coolly belonging to SC category. The family strived hard to meet livelihood. He succeeded in the 4th attempt and got 102nd Rank in civils. He secured 2nd class in 10th and Inter. In Degree and PG he got I class. He underwent training at AP study circle for I.A.S.

When he failed in the first attempt, friends discouraged him to try for civils. But all of them are unsuccessful candidates. Those who succeeded encouraged him. Mr. Bharat Bhusan an IRTS officer in Railways encouraged him. He supported financially. He is the role model for him.

Mr. K.K. Paul Board interviewed Mr. Vijaya Rao for 40 mts. Anthropology and Telugu literature are his optionals. More questions were on anthropology. The valley of questions include – duties of civil servants, free legal aid, Indo-Pak Relations, Red cross Society, J & K issue, Broad band connection, Semi Conductors and Solar System. **"Attempt honestly success is yours"** – is his advise.

Indian Forest Service Topper 2009

It is unbelievable. An young man is successful to make it true. We read in novels and watch in cinemas such type of success stories. Dedication, hard work and relentless efforts are milestones for success. He proved it. He scored 1st rank in Indian Forest Service in 2009. He is an example for the rural youth and poor. He topped the list. He is Mr. Sangram Kesari Behra.

He hails from a down trodden family. He studied over coming all the difficulties. He met with several experiences. The father of Mr. Sangram was running a barber shop. Sangram appeared for 2009 IFS exams and surprised every one by topping the list. He never blamed his lower strata for his failures. It is an eye opener for others. He is proud of his success. According to him economic status or poverty is not a hurdle for success in life. He hails from old Berhampur in Orissa State.

Mr. Naveen Patnaik, the Chief Minister of Orissa appreciated at his success and congratulated Mr. Sangram. He complemented him by praising it as a proud successful occasion for the entire Orissa. Mr. Sangram is a Post graduate in Zoology from Berhampur University. While continuing his studies he worked hard for IFS examinations.

He completed MSc in 2008 and the next year he topped in IFS. He won gold medal in MSc Zoology. He attempted IFS in 2008 unsuccessfully.

Next year when he topped the list the teaching staff of the university was overwhelmed with joy. He attempted civil services but the failure made him strong and determined. He mentioned it in a interview to the press.

"One or two failures increased my determination and with great dedication I succeeded in the examination. That is the only reason for my success".

He will try to help the people who have come from lower strata and will help in bringing up the society.

Winners' Views

Mr. A. Ramesh Reddy, IPS 2010.

> **"Everybody laughs at me; because I am different from them. But I laugh at all of them. Because all of them are same". – Said Albert Eienston.**

This is exactly correct in respect of Civils preparation in three stages, particularly with regard to prelims. This examination is like a visa for other stages. In this backdrop there are several misconceptions. Better to overcome them. The following are the misconceptions –

(1) **Vast Syllabus :** This is a wide spread idea. But the syllabus of the subject is defined in the notification very clearly. Keep syllabus copy with you during preparations.

(2) **Don't depend on a single material:** This is perfectly correct. Since the matter is so detailed better to read more than one book.

(3) **Difficult to remember everything:** This is 100% correct. When it is clearly known that concerned matter is only to be studied, why all the books available in the market are to be read.

Based on the notification issued in January and the examinations conducted in May, hardly 150 days are left for studies. Study for 100 days and allot 50 days for practice tests.

(4) **It is difficult to study 15 hours:** Serious study is most important than how many more number of hours you have studied. It is more important about your grasp on the subject.

Seven steps for preparation:

(1) Read previous question papers of each subject and prepare notes with important points.

(2) Read carefully all the questions after each chapter.

(3) Prepare notes with terminology of each subjects.

(4) Allot 30% of time for revision.

(5) Take practice test every day. Answer 20 questions atleast.

(6) Acquaint your self with current affairs through daily news papers.

(7) Maintain good health. Practice yoga. Sleep for seven hours a day. Sixteen to seventeen hours of preparation is needed.

Important things subject wise:

Geography: Read facts and concepts carefully. Based on previous question papers practice map pointing. Be thorough with the information regarding – population, census, weather, resources and details of various institutions. 25 to 30 questions from this wing will be given.

Polity: 12 questions in this chapter. Articles, schedules and amendments in constitutions, eligibility for appointments, important topics, connected with public affairs are to be studied.

Economy : Budget, different heads in budget, government projects, statistics regarding food production, industrial production, foreign exchange, credit balances, five year plans – are important subjects. Economic terminology and primary information is available in NCERT books. 10 to 15 questions are expected.

History: Ancient, medieval, modern history to be studied. Major events in Indian history – wars, dates, historical monuments, culture, poets and their contribution to literature. Royal patronage, important religious cults, are to be studied.

Current Events : Important conferences, meetings, awards, major calamities, indo-foreign relations, visits of Prime Minister and President of India to other countries, MOUs with different countries, important sports events – winners of world records, nobel prize winners, literary awards, latest book releases etc. 30 to 40 questions are expected.

Science and Technology : Basic knowledge of biology, physics, chemistry, new inventions, environmental issues, important seminars, institutions, new technologies – Nano technology, Bio-technology, Genetic Engineering etc. – 10 to 15 questions are probable.

Reference books :

(1) NCERT books of 8th to 12th class.
(2) Indian year book - Publications division, Delhi
(3) Old question papers.
(4) Standard Atlas.
(5) Analysis of current affairs.
(6) Spectrum prelim books.
(7) Manorama year book.

Above all confidence is the most vital point. Start with high ideas. **The long marathon race starts with first step only**. Change in life is necessary. Then try for better position with hard work and disciplined life.

Mr. V. Vinay Chand, IAS, Assistant Collector, Warangal, A.P. (2010)

The opinions expressed by Mr. Vinay Chand are interesting :

"It is widely known that among the optionals public administration is crazy. Candidates with sciences and Engineering background also opt for public administration. In optional question papers each question has 2.5 marks. Hence, one should be alert. The following strategies are suggested in public administration :

(1) Study the entire syllabus thoroughly.

(2) Study the last three years question papers to note down IMP points.

(3) In the prelims 12 chapters in public administration are prescribed. The questions will be only from these chapters. So don't waste time in collection of material.

(4) Among the 12 chapters, 4 chapters – public administration principles and theory are important. Among the total 120 questions, 40 to 50 questions are from this. The questions will be indirect and confuse the candidates. Study carefully.

(5) Read 1 or 2 standard books for these chapters. Take the advise of Seniors and Lecturers.

(6) The 10th Chapter containing information about union government, different provisions in constitution, local self government, Panchayat Raj system are very important.

(7) It is important to know underlying current and the view point of the writer.

(8) At the field level how these provisions can be implemented is to be noted. Have a clear understanding.

(9) It is important to read new books on management policies. Better to read different authors on the same subject. Ex. Different authors express different views. Study them.

(10) Knowledge about current topics is also important. Report of Administrative reforms committee is to be studied. Know the changes.

(11) **Preparations:** Analyze every item logically. After completing the book reading once or twice go for the other book. Minimum of 10 hours preparation is necessary.

(12) Allot 45 to 50% time for general studies and 50 to 55% for optionals.

(13) Those who are attempting for civils shall focus their full time from March onwards on studies.

(14) Those who are preparing for civils shall get control on the subjects by March. Other wise concentrate from the angle of prelims.

(15) Don't answer by lottery method. Negative marking is there.

(16) If you have full control over concepts, you will be able to identify the correct answer from choice. As a result you will be able to answer by elimination process.

(17) After completing prelims if you are sure of success, get ready for mains from Day No. 1, without wasting time.

(18) In between prelims and mains you have four months. At least 10 hrs preparation per day is required.

(19) Above all determination is needed.

Reference Material

- New Horizons of Public Administration – Mohit Battacharya.
- Elements of Public Administration – Phadia and Phadia
- Public Adminstration for Civils Prelims – Lakshmi Kanth
- Constitution of India – D.D. Basu
- Indian Administration – R.K. Arora and Rajani Goyal
- Second Administrative Reforms Committee Recommendations.

Common Tips

- Allot time for revision at least one month in advance to exams. During the month note down points in a book on the items you does not have clear perception. After completion of revision look at them leisurely.
- To have an idea about your strengths in answering cultivate practice tests. Analyse yourself about wrong answering.
- Those who are preparing for the first time, shall concentrate on prelims than on mains.
- Read at least 4 years back question papers, Identify the questions with more weightage and spend more time for them. Plan accordingly.
- If you are reading more than one author on a given subject analyse their views.
- After completion of reading a concept, take down notes which will help at the time of revision.
- Preparation shall be to answer 100 % questions.

D. Prasanth Kumar Reddy

Success in Geography: Compared to other subjects Geography is different from others. Syllabus is vast. Importance is for scientific approach. But don't get frightened. If you succeed in prelims, it will be early to gain marks in Mains. To select Geography as a suoject one has to have an approach towards it. But do not take it as a subject on the advice of others, though your aptitude is different.

Some of the items are lengthy and you should not get bored. Try for self motivation techniques. Regarding preparation few points are suggested:

- In Geography many items are fact based
- You have to remember the names of several scholars, their success stories and theories.
- Understanding concepts is more important, If 4 views are given on a subject you have to choose correct answer. You shall be able to identify.
- More weightage is for physical geography and Indian geography. More questions are given on them. You shall have clear understanding.
- Human Geography is also vital.
- Don't' forget climatology. 30 questions are expected.
- Thought maintaining is also important. 15 to 20 questions are expected. It is based on the views and prefaces of different authors. Ex. How earth is formed, formation of sea etc.
- Another aspect is Geographical thought. It appears like easy and theory content is more. You have to spend more time but it is not difficult.
- Keep watch on current topics also. Ex. Drought, less rains, oil and gas resources, disputes related to river waters, housing schemes, seminars on environment, Copenhagan Summit etc.
- Read old question papers of last four years. Concentrate on more weightage topics and prepare well.
- Don't conceive the idea to leave some topics. Those who are attempting for the first time shall answer all 20 questions.
- When we compare the previous results, those who have answered at least 80 questions got into mains.
- If you have hold on Geography, you can score 25 to 30 marks in general studies.
- Last two weeks are to be kept for revision. In prelims preparation.

Reference Material

- NCERT – 6th to 12 class text books.
- Environmental Geography – Surwinder Singh
- Human Geography – Mazeed Hussain
- Evolution of Geography - do -
- Atlas – Orient Longman

ANNEXURE 2 UNION PUBLIC SERVICE COMMISSION

Programme Calender of Examinations Year 2011

S. No.	*Name of Examination*	*Date of Notification/ Last date for receipt of applications*	*Date of commencement of Examination and its duration*	*Minimum academic qualifications prescribed*	*Age limits*
1.	Combined Medical services Examination. 2010	11.09.2010 11.10.2010	11.01.2011 (One day)	M.B.B.S. Degree	Below 32 years as/on 01.01.2011
2.	Combined defense services examination (I), 2010	25.09.2010 25.10.2010	13.02.2010 (One day)	(i) For IMA and OTA: Degree of a recognized University or equivalent.	For IMA 19-24 years as on 01.01.2011
				(ii) For naval Academy: B.Sc. (with Physics & Mathematics) or Bachelor of Engineering.	For NA 19-22 years as on 01.01.2011
				(iii) For Air Force Academy: Degree of a recognized University (with Physics and Mathematics at 10+2 level) or Bachelor of Engineering.	For AFA 19-23 years as on 01.01.2011 For OTA 19-25 years as on 01.01.2011

(Contd.)

(Contd. Table)

S. No.	*Name of Examination*	*Date of Notification/ Last date for receipt of applications*	*Date of commencement of Examination and its duration*	*Minimum academic qualifications prescribed*	*Age limits*
3.	National Defense Academy and Naval Academy Examination (I) 2010	16.10.2010 15.11.2010	17.04.2011 (One day)	(i) For Army Wing of National Defense Academy: 12th Class pass of the 10+2 pattern of School Education or equivalent, examination conducted by a State Education Board or a University. (ii) For Air force and Naval Wings of NDA and for 10+2 (Executive Branch) Course at Naval Academy: 12th Class pass of the 10+2 pattern of School Education or equivalent with physics and Mathematics conducted by a State Education Board or a University.	16 ½ - 19 years as on 01.01.2011
4.	Civil Services (Preliminary) Examination 2011	19.02.2011 21.03.2011	12.06.2011 (One day)	A degree from a recognized University or equivalent.	21-30 years as on 01.08.2011

(Contd.)

(Contd. Table)

S.No.	*Name of Examination*	*Date of Notification/ Last date for receipt of applications*	*Date of commencement of Examination and its duration*	*Minimum academic qualifications prescribed*	*Age limits*
5.	Engineering Services Examination, 2011	25.12.2010 24.1.2010	15.5.2011 (Three days)	A degree in Engineering from a recognized university or equivalent. M.Sc Degree or its equivalent with wireless communications, Electronics, Radio Physics or Radio Engineering as special subject acceptable for certain Service/posts only.	21-30 years as on 01.08.2011
6.	Indian Forest Service Examination, 2011	12.3.2011 11.4.2011	9.7.2011 (Ten days)	A bachelor's degree with at least one of the subjects namely, animal Husbandry and veterinary science, Botany, chemistry, geology, mathematics, physics, statistics and zoology or a degree in agriculture or forestry or engineering of a recognized university or equivalent.	21-30 years as on 01.07.2011

(Contd.)

(Contd. Table)

S.No.	*Name of Examination*	*Date of Notification/ Last date for receipt of applications*	*Date of commencement of Examination and its duration*	*Minimum academic qualifications prescribed*	*Age limits*
7.	SCRA Exam 2011	19.3.2011 19.04.2010	22.08.2011 (One day)	-	-
8.	NDA&NA Exam (II) 2011	9.04.2011 9.05.200	21.08.2011 (Seven days)	-	-
9.	National Defense Academy & Naval Academy Examination (II), 2010	09.04.2011 09.05.2011	21.08.2011 (One day)	(i) For any wing of National Defense Academy: 12th Class pass of the 10+2 pattern of School Education or equivalent examination conducted by a State Education Board of a University. (ii) For Air force and naval wings of NDA and for 10+2 (Executive Branch) Course at Naval Academy: 12th Class pass of the 10+2 pattern of school education or equivalent with physics and mathematics conducted by a State Education Board of a University.	16 ½ - 19 years as 01.07.2011

(Contd.)

(Contd. Table)

S.No.	*Name of Examination*	*Date of Notification/ Last date for receipt of applications*	*Date of commencement of Examination and its duration*	*Minimum academic qualifications prescribed*	*Age limits*
10.	Combined Defense services examination (II), 2010	30.4.2011 30.5.2011	18.09.2011 (One day)	(i) For IMA and OTA: Degree of a recognized University or equivalent.	For IMA 19-24 years as on 01.07.2011
				ii) For Naval Academy: B.Sc (with Physics and Mathematics) or Bachelor of Engineering.	For NA 19-22 years as on 01.07.2011
				iii) For Air Force Academy: Degree of a recognized University (with Physics and Mathematics at 10+2 level) or Bachelor of Engineering.	For AFA 19-23 years as on 01.07.2011 For OTA 19-25 years as on 01.07.2011
11.	Central Police Forces (Assistant Commandants) Examination, 2011	25.05.2011 27.06.2011	09.10.2011 (One day)	A degree from a recognized university or equivalent.	20-25 years as on 01.08.2011

(Contd.)

(Contd. Table)

S.No.	*Name of Examination*	*Date of Notification/ Last date for receipt of applications*	*Date of commencement of Examination and its duration*	*Minimum academic qualifications prescribed*	*Age limits*
12.	Civil Services (Main) Examination 2010		29.10.2011 (Twenty-one days)	A degree from a recognized University or equivalent.	21-30 years as on 01.08.2011
13.	Indian Economic/Indian Statistical Service Examination. 2010	30.07.2011 29.08.2011	13.12.2011 (Three days)	A Post-graduate degree in Economics/applied Economics/Business Economics/Econometrics for the IES and a Post-graduate degree in Statistics/Mathematical Statistics/Applied Statistics for the ISS, from a recognized University or equivalent.	21-32 years as on 01.01.201a.

(Contd.)

(Contd. Table)

S.No.	*Name of Examination*	*Date of Notification/ Last date for receipt of applications*	*Date of commencement of Examination and its duration*	*Minimum academic qualifications prescribed*	*Age limits*
14.	Geologists' Examination, 2010	13.08.2011 12.09.2011	03.12.2011 (Three days)	Master's Degree in Geology or Applied Geology or Marine Geology from a recognized University or equivalent.	21-32 years as on 01.01.2011
15.	Section officers / Stenographers' (grade "B" Grade-I) Limited Departmental Competitive Examination	23.07.2011 19.09.2011	17.12.2011 (Four days)		

ANNEXURE III
STUDIES ABROAD
Scholarships Calendar

January

Charles Walles Scholarships

To whom : Persons intending to do research work in UK for 3 to 4 weeks and to make professional visits.

No. of scholarships available: 15 annually

Eligibility: Age 25 to 40 years (Indian citizens)

Besides English knowledge, 4 or 5 years research experience after completion of academic studies.

Preference will be given for post Doctoral Research.

www.britishcouncil.org

February

INLAKS Scholarships

To whom : Students desirous to pursue higher studies in Europe or USA. (Confirmed Admission in those universities required)

Subjects : Engineering, computer Science, Urban planning, Business studies, medicine, public health, Indian studies and History.

No. of Scholarships : Maximum 10

Tuition fees, Expenditure towards rentals, one Air fare, will be released at the first instance.

Eligibility : Indian citizen's with Degree from a recognized University. Age : 30 years before 1st July.

Preference to candidates going abroad for the first time.

www.inlaksfoundation.org

or

Sivadasani Foundation
C/o. Inlaks India foundation, 86/87 Atlanta
Nariman Point, Mumbai 400 021.

Jawaharlal Nehru Memorial Trust Scholarships

To whom : Those who want to enroll for Ph.D. /Post Doctoral courses in UK in micro Electronics, computer sciences, Biotechnology, Economics, Mass communication and Management.

Air Fares will be reimbursed.

Eligibility : Below 30 years. Master Degree/ Ph.D.

Experience of 2 years in Research/Training.

Last Date : March 15th

Applications to : Secretary, Dept of Education,
External scholarship Division
A -1/W3, Curzan Road Barracks,
Kasturba Gandhi marg, New Delhi 110001

K.C. Mahindra Scholarships

To whom : To join in PG courses in Engineering, Natural sciences, Humanities, Medicine, Business Management, Military, Naval and Aviation Sciences.

Eligibility : Degree or Diploma from recognized university in the concerned subject with I class marks.

Conformation of seat from established foreign universities required.

Rs.90,000 as scholarship will be given for the selected candidates.

www.mahindra.com

Scholarship for studies in Mexico

To whom : P.G. and above studies in Mexico in Spanish History, literature, linguistics, Demography, Asia and Africa studies etc.

Scholarship for 1 to 2 yrs will be granted besides reimbursement of Tuition fee, Medical insurance and Accommodation rentals.

Eligibility : P.G. Degree or Ph.D.

Age : Below 45 yrs.

The candidate on return to India after studies shall work for a minimum of 2 years in India.

March

Commonwealth Scholarship / Fellowships in UK

To whom : For research in UK in Medicine, Engineering, Technologies, Sciences, Agricultural, Allied subjects, Humanities, Social Sciences etc.

For Master Degree : 1 year

For Ph.D. Degree 3 years scholarships will be given.

Candidates for Project oriented Training shall only apply and not for Degrees.

Eligibility : Those who applied for masters Degree.

Those who scored minimum of 55% in Bachelor Degree in Sciences and 60% in others. Similarly in P.G. also.

www.britishcouncil.org

Fullbright Nehru's masters fellowship for leadership development

To whom : For those who are applying for professional studies in Business Administration, Communication studies, Economics, Enrichment & Public Administration. The Advertisement appears in Feb/March.

Eligibility : 4 yrs Degree course equivalent to US Bachelor Degree from Recognized Universities or Masters Degree.

Experience for 3 yrs in leadership and community services

www.USIEF.org.in/Scripts/

April

Agatha Harrison Memorial Fellowship

(Saint Antonys College, Oxford)

To whom : Scholars doing advanced research in Oxford University in History, Economics, Political Science, Master Studies etc.

Scholarship : 24536 pounds in I year. Next year onwards it increases.

Eligibility : Indians between 30 and 40 years

60% in master degree/ Ph.D.

Teaching experience for 3 years for graduate/ PG Students.

www.education.nic.in

HRD Scholarships for Japan

To whom : for students of Ph.D. in Japan in Information Technology, optical fiber communication, quality and reliability engineering, electronics, and telecommunications, laser technology, bio technology, Japanese language and literature, fisheries, Japanese studies, earth quake engineering, environmental studies, architecture, aero space engineering and material sciences etc.

Scholarships will be given for 18 to 24 months for 35 candidates.

Eligibility : 60 % marks in concerned subjects in PG.

Practical research/ Teaching / work experience.

www.education.nic.in

Research Scholarships in Turkey

To whom : For students of research in recognized university of Turkey in agriculture, bio technology, environmental engineering.

Scholarships equivalent to Rs. 6000/- will be given.
60 % marks in PG course.
Proficiency in English and French/ Turkey Language
Eligibility : Those who have completed degree 4 years back.
www.education.nic.in

May

Mexican Scholarships

To whom : For candidates of PG /Ph.D. courses in Mexico in Agriculture, Architecture, Bio technology, Environment Sciences, Psychology, Geography etc.

Eligibility : 26 years for P.G. Students.
30 years for Ph.D. Students.
60% in Bachelor Degree and 65% in PG. for Ph.D.
www.education.nic.in

Rotary Ambassadorial scholarships

To whom : For Students in PG/Ph.D./Post Doctoral studies in foreign countries. Preference for cultural studies and Regular academic studies.

Eligibility : 2 years course in college/ university
2 years experience in an industrial institution.
www.rotary.org

ITC overseas scholarships

To whom : For admission in stipulated institutions in business management, environment management, environment engineering in PG. courses.

Eligibility : 1st Class Bachelors Degree. Duties in development policy institutions, Government bodies.
Last Date : October
www.newdelhi.daad.de/mainframe/home

Rhodes Scholarships

To whom : For candidates who obtained admission for master degree of Oxford University
Scholarship for 2 years

Eligibility : Degree with 1st Class.
www.rhodesscholarshipsindia.com

Australian Endeavour Scholarships

To whom : To the students admitted in vocational courses, research and professional courses in Australia.

Eligibility : 1st class marks in Bachelor / PG courses

10 years experience for under graduates and

5 years for post graduates

www.endeavour.deewr.gov.au.

August

Charles Wallace scholarships

To whom : Candidates admitted in different institutes in UK

- Writer fellowships – 3 months – university of Kent.
- Writer fellowships – 3 months – center for common wealth studies, University of Sterling.
- Translator fellowships – 2 months – British center for literary translation, University of Anglia.

Eligibility : Between 25 to 45 years

No age limit for translator fellowships

Master's Degree or 5 to 7 years experience

www.britishcouncil.org.indianscholarshipcwit.htm

September

Schol Scholarship, Oxford

To whom : Students seeking admission for M.B.A.

Last date Sept – Oct.

Eligibility : Experience in social ventures for 1 year

www.sbs.ox.ac.uk

Chinese Scholarships

To whom : For admission in P.G. courses in Chinese language and literature and sciences etc.

Scholarship for 1 to 4 years.

Eligibility : Below 40 years

60 % marks in UG for PG students

www.education.nic.in

HRD Scholarships – Norway

To whom : PG / M.Phil. in natural resources, Developmental studies etc.

Scholarships for 10 months.

For PG students 8000 Norway crowns

For Ph.D. students : 11500 Norway crowns

Eligibility : 60 % marks in PG, below 40 years.

Confirmation letter from Norway institute is required.

www.education.nic.in

October

The great Cambridge Scholarships

To whom : Students of PG/ Research in Cambridge university.

90 scholarships per year

Eligibility : I or High second class marks in Hons. Degree.

www.gatesschloar.org

Vanier Canada Scholarships

To whom : For Doctoral studies in 92 universities of Canada

50000 Canadian dollars per year for 3 years.

Eligibility : Good academic record, teaching experience etc.

www.vanier.gc.ca

Ford foundation post doctoral research fellowships in economics

To whom : Students of post doctoral research in recognized universities.

Scholarship for 1 year

Eligibility : Teachers in colleges / universities below 40 years.

www.ifpsa.org

November

Check Republic Scholarships

To whom : Students of PG/Ph.D. in Electronics, Electrical, Mechanical Engineering.

Master Degree – 7000 crowns.

Ph.D. Students – 7500 crowns.

Eligibility : 60% marks in bachelor / PG courses.

www.education.nic.in

ADB (Asian Development Bank) Japan Scholarships

To whom : Citizens of ADB member countries seeking admission in Economics, Commerce, Engineering etc.

Scholarships in the form of tuition fees, medical insurance etc.

Eligibility : 60 % marks through out academic career with 2 yrs experience.

www.adb.org.jsp

December

Dr. Manmohan Singh Scholarships

To whom : Students admitted in Cambridge university

Eligibility : Bachelor or Master Degree – Below 35 years

www.britishcouncil.org

Case Study

Mr. Y. Reddy Sekhar, 28 years hails from a village – Gurram Konda in chittoor District, Andhra Pradesh. His father is a peasant. Reddy sekhar did his P.G. in Anthropology in 2006 from university of Hyderabad. Later he completed his M.Phil from Pondichery university on health practices in tribal areas–with special reference to NOKRAI Village (East Godavari District, A.P.).

He was interested in doing research abroad. He has published research papers in Cam bridge journal and was watching different websites for scholarships abroad. With the guidance of Professor ROBIN OKLAY his application was processed and admitted for Doctoral research in Anthropology about health practices at Dalhousie University. Canada in 2009 for 5 years.

He got fellowships worth 10 lacks in Indian Rupees. Students should watch for opportunities and take the help of Professors. Normally students does not bother to collect information regarding foreign studies

OTHER COURSES IN INDIA

NET Examinations by University Grants Commission (UGC)

The examinations are conducted by UGC for eligibility for appointments as lecturers in universities and colleges. The examinations are conducted twice a year – June and December.

Eligibility : Any PG degree with 50% marks

The examination is conducted in 3 papers

Paper I. General Studies – 150 marks

Paper II. Subject 1 – 150 marks.

Paper III Subject 2 – 300 marks.

Subject 1 - contains objective questions of one mark each.

Subject 2 – Descriptive questions – Answers type.

There will be questions for 40 marks, 20 marks and 5 marks.

Candidates who score 60% and above marks are eligible for Junior Research fellowships.

Persons with Below 60% marks are eligible for appointment as lecturer. If a candidate is pursuing M.Phil/Ph.D. and got 60% and above in NET he will get a monthly fellowship of Rs. 12000/-

AIEEA PG : Examinations – April every year

Eligibility : Bachelors Degree in Agriculture (10+2+3/4/5)

For MVSC admission: BVSC Degree

Institutes Offering Courses : ICAR, Indian veterinary Research institute, Central institute of Fisheries education, NDRI (100% seats)

25% seats allotted in state Agri Universities, B.H.U, Viswabharathi and Nagaland Univ.

Exam Pattern : 650 marks with multiple choice in concerned subjects with cross matching. 150 questions with multiple choice – 4 marks each. Matching – 10 questions with 5 sub questions – 1 mark each = 50 : Total 650 marks.

For wrong answer 0.2 marks negative marking (in cross matching)

Jr.AF : 475 Junior Research Fellowships in 20 subjects. Selected candidates will get fellowship of Rs. 8640 per month in other subjects and Rs. 12000 per month for veterinary science candidates.

Job Opportunities : Those who complete subjects related to Agriculture will get jobs in Public and Private sectors. They can appear for the prestigious IFS (Indian Forest Service Examinations). Corporate institutions like Rallys, Monosanto, ITC, Andhra Bank, OBC, Bank of Baroda, recruit PG degree holders with agricultural background. Different research institutes and laboratories also absorb them. Excellent job opportunities abroad are also available.

The application can be down loaded from website –

www. icar. org.in

Last date – February every year.

AIEEA for Agricultural Courses

India is an agrarian country. Govt gives preference for Agriculture. So Agriculture education and research has lot of priority, to cater to the needs of agro based industries. Youth has lot of opportunities in agro based industries.

Acharya NG. Ranga Agricultural University at Hyderabad offer U.G., P.G.and Ph.D. courses. For admission into graduate courses (B.Sc. Ag) EMACET combined entrance test in May every year is conducted by different states. At the national level Indian Council for Agricultural Research (ICAR- an independent organization under ministry of

Agriculture) conducts entrance test for graduate and post graduate courses (AIEEA – UG and AIEEA PG). Successful candidates are admitted in State agricultural universities (15% quota) and 100% in National dairy research institute (NDRI) and ICAR.

Institutions offering PG Courses in Journalism

1. Bharatiya Vidya Bhavan : All centers of Bharatiya Vidya Bhavan offer PG diplomas in Journalism and Mass Communication – Part time – 1 year.
2. A.P.J. Institute of Mass Communication, Delhi.
   M.A. Journalism and Mass Communications
   Eligibility – 50% marks in Degree
   www.apeejay.edu
3. Makhanlal Chaturvedi University of Journalism and Mass com., Bhopal
   Master of Journalism – 2 years course
   M.A. Advertising and P.R., M.A. Broadcast Journalism.
   M.Sc Electronic Media, M.A. Mass com.
   Eligibility : Bachelors Degree and entrance test.
   www.mcu.ac.in
4. Asian College of Journalism, Chennai
   P.G. Diploma in Journalism (Photo Journalism optional)
   Eligibility: Degree & Entrance Test.
   www.asianmedia.org
5. Indira Gandhi National Open University (IGNOU) New Delhi.
   P.G. Diploma in Journalism
   Eligibility: Degree & Experience in media
   www.ignou.ac.in
6. Osmania University, Hyderabad
   M.C.J. at PG level
   Eligibility: Bachelor of Communication and Journalism with 40% marks
   www.osmania.ac.in
7. Andhra University, Visakapatnam
   Master of Journalism and Mass Communication
   Eligibility: Degree/ M.A./M.Com
   www.andhrauniversity.info
8. Sri Padmavathi Mahila University, Tirupati
   M.C.J – 2 years

9. Nagarjuna University, Guntur
   M.A Journalism and Mass Communication – 1 year
   PG Dip. In Journalism and Mass Comm.
   Eligibility Degree.
   www.nagarjunauniversity.ac.in
10. P.S. Telugu University, Hyderabad
    Master of Communication and Journalism – 2 years
    Eligibility: Degree
    www.teluguuniversity.ac.in.
11. University of Hyderabad, Hyderabad
    MA Communications
    Eligibility: 55% Marks in Degree
    Entrance Test and Interview
    PG Dip. In Mass Com. and Translation Techniques.
    Medium : Urdu
    Eligibility : Degree
    www.uohyd.ernet.in.
12. Telangana University, Nizamabad, AP
    MA in Communications – 2 Yrs.
    Eligibility : Degree
13. Times School of Journalism, Delhi
    P.G. Dip. In Journalism – 1 Yr.
    Eligibiity: Degree with 50% Marks
    www.tcms.in
14. Moulana Azad National Urdu University, Hyderabad
    M.A. Mass Com. and Journalism (Urdu) – 2 yrs
    Eligibiity: Degree
    Candidates must have studied up to 10th or Inter in Urdu Medium.

Top 15 Journalism Colleges in India

1. Indian Institute of Mass Communication, New Delhi
2. Symboyasis Institute of Mass Comm., Pune
3. Mudra Institute of Communications, Ahmedabad.
4. A.J. Kidwai Mass Com. and Research Centre, Jamia, New Delhi.
5. Indian Institute of Journalism and News Media, Bangalore
6. Xavier Institute of Communication, Mumbai
7. Asian College of Journalism, Chennai
8. Film and Television Institute of India, Pune
9. Manorama School of Comm., Kottamyam
10. Times School Journalism, Delhi

11. A.P.J. Institutes of Mass Communication, Delhi
12. Institute of Mass Com. Film and T.V. Studies, Kolkata
13. Academy of Photo Graphic Excellence, New Delhi
14. Academy of Broadcasting, Chandigarh
15. Advertising Club, Tamil Nadu

Similarly several other Universities are also offering P.G. Courses in Journalism and Mass communications.

Index